HOW
to
SELL
to an
IDIOT

HOW
to
SELL
to an
IDIOT

12 Steps to Selling Anything to Anyone

JOHN HOOVER
BILL SPARKMAN
"The Coach"

WILEY

John Wiley & Sons, Inc.

Published by John Wiley & Sons, Inc., Hoboken, New Jersey.
Published simultaneously in Canada.

For general information on our other products and services please contact our Customer Care Department within the United States at (800) 762-2974, outside the United States at (317) 572-3993 or fax (317) 572-4002.

Wiley also publishes its books in a variety of electronic formats. Some content that appears in print may not be available in electronic books. For more information about Wiley products, visit our web site at www.Wiley.com.

Library of Congress Cataloging-in-Publication Data:

Hoover, John, 1952–
     How to sell to an idiot : 12 steps to selling anything to anyone / John Hoover, Bill Sparkman "The Coach".
       p. cm.
     ISBN-13 978-0-471-71854-3 (pbk.)
     ISBN-10 0-471-71854-8 (pbk.)
     1. Selling—Psychological aspects. I. Sparkman, Bill, 1948– II. Title.
HF5438.8.P75.H66 2006
658.85—dc22

                                                                    2005006847

Printed in the United States of America.

10   9   8   7   6   5   4   3   2   1

CONTENTS

ABOUT THE
AUTHORS

John Hoover, PhD, is an organizational behavior specialist, author, consultant, and a popular speaker and seminar personality. He is a former executive with the Disneyland Entertainment Division and, as managing partner of the second firm in the United States to publish commercial audiobooks, he wrote and produced works featuring authors including Herbert Benson, Ken Blanchard, Harold Bloomfield, Jack Canfield, Danny Cox, Terrance Deal, Peter F. Drucker, Dean Edell, Lillian Glass, Mark Victor Hansen, Tom Hopkins, Irene Kassorla, Norman Vincent Peale, Larry Peter, Al Ries, Robert H. Schuller, Jack Trout, and Zig Ziglar. Since selling his audio/video publishing company to McGraw-Hill and serving three years as general manager of McGraw-Hill's audio and video publishing, he has consulted on a wide variety of projects for clients including Boeing, Delta Air Lines, Hilton Hotels, IBM, Motorola, Printronix, Sanyo Fisher, and Xerox.

Dr. John has authored or coauthored eight books prior to *How to Sell to an Idiot*. Time permitting, he teaches classes in business planning, communications, entrepreneurship, principles of management, and organizational behavior as an adjunct faculty member at several colleges and universities in Tennessee. He is cofounder, with

Angelo Valenti, PhD, of the *ComposiTEAM Leadership System,* a new system for aligning the composite personalities of teams with projects, assignments, and initiatives to enhance and accelerate performance.

Dr. John is also partnered with Roger P. DiSilvestro to teach the Art of Constructive Confrontation to businesses of all sizes, including not-for-profits and government agencies at www.constructive confrontation.com. His background also includes several years as a California Board of Behavioral Sciences-registered marriage, family, and child counseling intern, street gang counselor for the Orange County Probation Department, and life skills counselor for homeless families in transition and adolescents in crisis. Dr. John is a Tennessee Supreme Court Rule 31 civil mediator.

He belongs to the American Society of Training and Development, the Organization Development Network, and the Society for Human Resources Management. Dr. John holds a Master of Arts degree in Marriage and Family Therapy from Azusa Pacific University in addition to his master of arts and doctorate degrees in Human and Organization Development from the Fielding Institute in Santa Barbara, California. Previous books Dr. John has authored, coauthored, or ghosted include:

- *The Art of Constructive Confrontation: How to Achieve More Accountability with Less Conflict* (Wiley, 2005) with Roger DiSilvestro
- *Unleashing Leadership: Aligning What People Do Best with What Organizations Need Most* (Career Press, 2005) with Angelo Valenti
- *How to Live with an Idiot: Clueless Creatures and the People Who Love Them* (Career Press, 2004)
- *How to Work for an Idiot: Survive and Thrive without Killing Your Boss* (Career Press, 2003).
- *Leadership When the Heat's On* (2nd ed.; McGraw-Hill, 2002) with Danny Cox
- *Think Out of the Box!* for Mike Vance and Diane Deacon (Career Press, 1995)

- *Seize the Day: How to Be an Extraordinary Person in an Ordinary World* (Career Press, 1994) with Danny Cox
- *An American Quality Legend: How Maytag Saved Our Moms, Vexed the Competition, and Pre-saged the Quality Revolution* (McGraw-Hill, 1993) with Robert J. Hoover

Bill Sparkman is a professional speaker, sales trainer, and sales coach. He has been speaking to, training, and coaching individuals and companies to success since 1987. Bill is the creator of Total Success Seminars. His nuts-and-bolts, real-world approach to learning and increasing personal performance has helped others move quickly to new levels of achievement.

Bill's background in the world of sports, as a player and coach, as well as his experience directing and leading the sales and marketing efforts of a billion-dollar-a-year corporation, has given him real-time experience that all of his audiences benefit from immediately. Bill believes that "Success is not an accident," it is a choice—a choice that literally thousands of his students have made over the years, with his guidance.

His "How to Sell to an Idiot" seminar can be presented for your sales team in half- or full-day sessions. Bill and Dr. John are available for keynote presentations for your group's next event. Your team will acquire a step-by-step strategy on how to get from "Hello" to "Where do I sign?" in record time. To schedule this powerful seminar, e-mail Bill or John at billthecoach@att.net or drjohnhoover@comcast.net. The coach looks forward to hearing from you. Until then, keep winning!

Bill and Dr. John both send special thanks to Paula Chapin Hartford for her meticulous proofing of this manuscript.

PREFACE

Total success in selling does not come from a series of random events, manipulation, covert persuasion tactics, the "Ben Franklin" close, or the stars all lining up perfectly. For you to make the sale, you just have to be lucky. We believe that luck and success are achieved by design. Luck is a choice, and so is success. It's amazing how lucky you can get with the right attitude and by using the right tools.

High achievers in any field of business or life know that success is not a coincidence: It is a series of concrete steps and right decisions made on a daily basis, or even more frequently. If you are seeking to change your results, it is going to take more than new goals, a new, positive attitude, or a brand-new suit. It is going to take new action on your part. New ideas alone just won't get it done. There are lots of positive-thinking, goal-setting underachievers, with everything going for them except one thing; a signature at the bottom of the contract. A master salesperson has the ability to match insight with action. Your willingness to try new strategies and continually challenge yourself will make new results possible and keep the window of opportunity open.

If you're not getting the results that you want, or if you are looking to accelerate the pace of your results, it may be the perfect time to call a time-out and make some adjustments to your current sales system. Making adjustments is different from scrapping your entire approach. There are really only two ways to fail in sales—doing things that don't work, and not doing things that do work. Do more of those things that are working for you and less of what's not working for you. Then incorporate things that are working for others into your daily routine. It sounds simple—but if it is so simple, why are there so many people doing what doesn't work for them and expecting different results? Sometimes working harder and harder at achieving what you want moves you further away from getting it. It may be time to de-complicate the entire selling process. Make it easy for customers to buy. Everything you do should simplify your customers' decisions. After all, they're not rocket scientists.

Speaking of keeping it simple, have you ever tried telling a four-year-old "No"? Some of the greatest salespeople on this planet are between the ages of three and eight. The natural sales skills of kids were not learned at some sales boot camp. You've had the sales skills required to get the results you want all along. You've just forgotten most of them. If you are not using these natural skills, they've been replaced by some things that you may want to unlearn.

Kids have a simplistic approach to getting what they want. They ask for it and keep asking until they get it. They have a very high tolerance for the word "No." Kids reject rejection. When they are told "No," they don't hang their heads or take it personally. They just regroup and get more creative. Kids have a great work ethic. They don't seem to wear down until they get what they want; a lesson that could be learned by those who underachieve in the sales biz. Kids have goals. They know how to negotiate. Their follow-up skills and persistence are unmatched by even some of the highest producers of the world's greatest sales forces.

Some of today's greatest sales trainers are right in front of you at the park or skateboarding down your driveway. Take time to watch them, listen to them, and take good notes. They may help remind you of all the skills you once used to acquire exactly what you truly desired. This book presents a balance between learning new skills and strategies and unlearning those things that are blocking you or holding you back. Selling to and winning over your toughest customer is a matter of creating your luck by developing practical, concrete steps to producing a sale that's a positive experience for your customer. It's also a matter of being willing to change and adjust your approach, and de-complicating the entire process by utilizing those skills and tools used by some of the greatest salespeople in the world—kids.

INTRODUCTION

How to Sell to an Idiot is an opportunity to lighten up a little and learn a lot. Successful selling is largely a matter of attitude—yours. The right attitude will float you from, "Hello, my name is Fred," to a signature on an order. Nevertheless, most sales professionals still make the fatal error of underestimating their customers. If you think your customers are idiots you might be right some of the time. But sales professionals who stop there will come up short most of the time. While some are pointing fingers and snickering at their idiot customers, others will be getting the idiot's signature on an order. An idiot's dollar buys just as much as William F. Buckley's dollar.

Our definition of an idiot: one who hasn't a clue. Meet the clueless. Customers can be clueless simply because they don't know what they don't know. That's why it's your job to be a great teacher. Then again, you might be just as clueless, because *you* don't know what you don't know. Your clueless customers, however, don't have the slightest inclination, desire, responsibility, or motivation to teach you anything.

It's your job to learn from them so you'll know what you need to teach. Be pro-intentional. Your idiot customers (*i*-customers) will remain blissfully clueless until some sales professional comes along and takes the time and exerts the effort and resources to enlighten them. We hope that sales professional will be you.

The ability to fool some of the people some of the time isn't what helps the greatest sales professionals to enjoy lucrative rewards over the long haul. Super-sellers have discovered where and how their life experiences and expectations resonate with their customers' life experiences and expectations. When that happens, you sell and your customers buy—all with greater confidence. That shouldn't be too hard if you're selling to idiots, right?

Wrong. One of the primary reasons sales professionals don't reach their goals is because they forget to account for the biggest idiot of all. Meet your inner idiot. Every one of us can get so wrapped up in trying to outmaneuver others that we ignore our own cluelessness, and our best-laid plans suffer as a result. If the defining characteristic of an idiot is cluelessness, the challenge for sales professionals is to surgically implant enough of a clue in their *i*-customers to ensure they reach the correct buying decision.

True sales professionals accept that they have inner idiots, and work to ensure their own clues are intact first. The greatest success you can experience in dealing with others occurs when your inner idiot connects with the cluelessness in the other person and you're able to make him or her feel better about him- or herself. That's much of what *How to Sell to an Idiot* is about: emotional selling.

Everybody has feelings. Don't be afraid to use yours. No matter how clueless potential customers might be, they're not going to buy anything from you unless they believe they're going to feel good about it afterwards. That puts the ball squarely in your court—to make sure that customers feel their purchases are safe, sensible, and self-enhancing. The ability to consistently make people feel good about their purchasing decisions pays enormous dividends. Finding out what makes people feel comfortable and delivering for them time after time is the key that unlocks the exceptional payoffs all sales professionals dream about.

Selling to an idiot isn't difficult as long as your inner idiot is not in charge. Don't blame your idiot customer if you can't close the sale. Selling to a genius will be a disaster if your inner idiot is in charge. Because of the natural power advantage a current or prospective customer (idiot or genius) has over the sales professional, superior knowledge, ability to communicate, persistence, and passion are among the requirements needed to bridge the gap. Practicing the specific skills described in this and every other book ever written on the art and craft of salesmanship will sharpen your scalpel and put you in the driver's seat, no matter how bright or dull your customers are, or, more importantly, how bright or dull you are on any given day.

Tough customers are nothing more than a reminder that you have more to learn. You have more to learn about them and more to learn about yourself. Learning about one does no good without learning about the other. At some point and at some level your inner idiot and your customer's inner idiot share the same space in the universe. That's the place from which to begin applying all of the natural and acquired talent and knowledge you continue to accumulate and refine.

Many times, the tougher that customers are to close, the more they're likely to buy. They just want to know if you're really serious. Just how serious you are is up to you. The critical path to selling to the clueless is a 12-step process. Each step builds on the prior step, gaining strength and momentum along the way. Skipping steps or trying to shortcut the system diminishes the effectiveness of the ultimate results—perhaps even spelling the difference between success and failure. Follow the plan and, when in doubt, imitate the work of the world's greatest salespeople: kids. Most of the time kids think we're idiots. However, they get what they want with amazing consistency, using a mixture of unparalleled creativity and sheer tenacity.

The many and often quirky personality types you encounter in your sales career include the Machiavellians, the sadists, the masochists, the paranoids, the Greek gods and goddesses, the emotionally needy, and the honestly decent souls. Dealing with some of your more outrageous customers requires learning to speak new languages. Depending on what you're selling and who you're selling to, you might want to add Klingon to your vocabulary. Seriously folks, check out the Klingon Language Institute at www.kli.org. Their money is as green as a Young Republican's.

At the end of the day, to be the great salesperson you've always dreamt of being, and to acquire all of the possessions, influence, and/or success you've dreamt of acquiring, you need to learn the language and the lifestyles of the clueless, accept and make good use of the cluelessness within yourself, embrace the emotional power in selling, become a great teacher, follow the 12 steps described in this book, accept and adapt to the unique personalities you'll encounter, and do it all with the tenacity and relentless determination of a child. Bring your sense of humor and let's begin.

HOW
to
SELL
to an
IDIOT

1

STEP ONE:
BE PREPARED
OR BE THE IDIOT

A professional salesperson is always prospecting. Prospecting is being alert for clues. The first clue you need to uncover is, "Am I dealing with a prospect or a suspect?" If you merely suspect a customer might buy, you're leaving too much to chance. Start every day right by visualizing everyone you encounter as a prospective or potential customer. Even your current customers have the potential to buy more. Some customers will have more buying potential than others: desire, need, or appropriateness for the goods and/or services you're selling, ability to pay, and awareness of how much he or she will benefit from the purchase.

All of the preceding notwithstanding, any potential or current customer might be an idiot or not. In the end, it doesn't matter. Idiot or genius, their money is worth the same amount once it hits the bank. It's up to you to be pro-intentional enough to make sure someone else doesn't sell them what you're selling and take their money to another bank—which would make you the idiot.

Sales professionals who set out each day to find suckers are starting on the wrong foot, and will probably trip over or stick it in their mouth before the day is through. Your prospecting and potential-finding will ultimately pay off in direct proportion to how skilled you are and how honestly you go about it. Prospecting is a state of mind. You need to believe from your head to your toes that what you have to offer others is so helpful, valuable, and beneficial that your current and prospective customers would be fools not to buy. If you don't believe that, chances are that you'll wind up making those who do buy from you look and feel like fools for becoming your customers.

NEED AND INTENT

You don't need Coach Bill or Dr. John to tuck you in and read you to sleep from the volumes that have been written about sales prospecting. What we will do is hit some prospecting highlights, as we reframe the concept enough to keep you from looking Looney Tunes in front of your prospects and peers. Authentic prospecting is a process of establishing need and intent. You and your prospects have needs and intentions. The intersection of those needs and intentions are where you make the big bucks.

To make sure you don't stand alone in that intersection, like a bride or groom abandoned at the altar, you must first understand why you're there. Is it to feed your family, buy that bass boat or Dodge Viper, take a cruise around the world, move into the Elvis suite at the Las Vegas Hilton—or all of the above? Those sound like wants more than needs—except for the feeding your family part. Orthodonture and college tuitions are getting more expensive, so we'll wager you're out there pounding the pavement for some combination of wants and needs, and it's your intention to fulfill those wants and needs for yourself and those who depend on you.

What makes you think anyone else is different? Your current and prospective customers are flapping their wings in the same airspace in which you're trying to fly. If they're not in the same intersection of needs and intentions that you occupy, you have two choices: (1) move to their intersection or (2) convince them to move to yours. If you truly believe from the top of your head to the tips of your toes that what you have to offer is so helpful, valuable, and beneficial that they would be fools not to buy, you'll do one or the other.

Other people's wants and needs might not exactly reflect or resonate with yours, but that doesn't mean they don't have equally powerful intentions to fulfill them. Being pro-intentional means finding the frequency they're tuned in to and transmitting your program on that same frequency. Understanding that there are wants, needs, and intentions as powerful as yours all around you is like being a radio station during drive time. There are lots of receivers out there for what you're broadcasting.

Nobody's an idiot merely because they aren't listening to you. You have other stations to compete with. The last thing you need to do is turn potential listeners off to radio altogether. You have enough forces in the universe working against you. No need to complicate your effort with lack of preparation and awareness. The hill you climb every day is steep enough. Why wear roller skates? The operative word in the phrase "The Right Stuff" is "Right." Being right in the sales business is usually synonymous with being ready.

MENTAL PREPARATION MADE SIMPLE
(OR MENTAL PREP FOR THE SIMPLE)

Translate need and intent into planning and preparation. Planning and preparation are important, but not so important that they become procrastination in disguise. Idiots are differentiated from nonidiots in the sales force by the way nonidiots make their plans pay off, while idiots use their planning and preparation to avoid selling. Idiots overplan, consciously or unconsciously giving themselves an excuse to accomplish nothing. Other idiots don't plan at all, thereby giving themselves an excuse to fail without guilt. They set no target to not hit.

As far as the idiot customer goes, lack of planning on his or her part can be your friend. You know what chaos feels like. You know how comforting it can be to hide inside the eye of the hurricane. Remember, intention is intention is intention—yours and your customers'. It's up to you to make your *i*-customers feel like you're a safe harbor in the storm, and to feel like what you're selling is the answer to their problems, the anchor to their happiness, the secret of the ages, the fountain of youth, the meaning of life, whatever.

As long as you believe in your solution with every molecule in your body, find someone being blown about by the storm and offer to pull them into the boat. When a potential customer is feeling disorganized, *carpe* the opportunity. By doing idiots' planning and preparation for them you can control the purpose and urgency of the sales encounter. If the customer is more organized than you are you'll look like an atmospheric disturbance to them—and they'll avoid you. That generates little confidence and few sales.

Don't get hung up on thinking we're being judgmental with the idiot thing. Good, well-intentioned people can be nonetheless clueless. We'll volunteer to top the list. The good news is that, as a sales professional, it's possible to work with mostly nice people who need your help filling in their blanks. Your goal is to help your prospective customer sense his or her wants and needs and develop the ongoing intention to seek you out for relief. You must learn to clue in on the clueless equivalent of a low-pressure system on The Weather Channel. Where there is a distinct absence of information, the opportunity is ripe to fill in the trough. When you're tempted to label someone an idiot, think of them instead as a new student, ready if not eager to learn something new . . . something you have to teach.

CHOOSING IN: THE CURE FOR CLUELESSNESS

Whether you're employed by a small, medium, or large firm—or you're completely self-employed—you're essentially in business for yourself. The talent, skill, and effectiveness you bring to your work every day determines the amount of reward and satisfaction you receive for your effort. Having said that, you have at least two choices you can make every day about your business. The first choice is to work less, think less, earn less, be less successful, and generally be happy less often. Choice number one also leads to diminished fulfillment, less rewarding results, and more stress. It's amazing how popular this choice is.

Behind door number two is the choice to have it all, do it all, be generally happy, and to earn as much as you possibly can. The people society calls winners—those who accomplish great things—virtually always choose door number two. The greatest rewards are reserved for those who accomplish great things. There's nothing idiotic about that. The idiotic thing is to try and shortcut and/or subvert time-proven formulas for success and expect somehow to experience success anyway.

The greatest rewards are reserved for those who consistently make the right choices. The key word here is "consistently." The right choice once in a while won't get it done. So, choose *in* every day. Let somebody else be the idiot. Your customers aren't idiots when it comes to feeling respected and cared for. In other words, as clueless as they might seem from time to time (for some all the time), they're always conscious at some level about the choices you make regarding your own success.

SIMPLE VERSUS EASY: THE INNER IDIOT REARS ITS UGLY HEAD

We wouldn't subject you to tired old rah-rah rhetoric about making the right choices, the big effort, or taking the high road if we didn't have a twist on the theme. The big mistake people make when attempting to increase sales performance is in equating "simple" with "easy." Everybody knows that successful selling is largely a numbers game. Your closing ratio is determined by a number of things. Perhaps the most significant of those is the number of times every day that you pick up the telephone or knock on a door to contact a potential customer or take care of an existing one.

If your closing ratio is 10 percent, every 10th call or knock, on average, will result in a sale. If your commission is 10 dollars for every sale, 10 percent might be a realistic ratio of cold calls to closings. If your commission is 100,000 dollars per sale, your ratio might be something more like 500 to 1, or more. You've no doubt determined how many closings it will take to live the lifestyle of your dreams. The math is simple, but the execution is not easy. "It's numbers, nothing more," you reason with yourself over and over. "What is so hard about this?"

If simple translates to easy, only the complicated will be hard. "Okay," you continue to negotiate with your inner idiot. (We all have one. Get used to it.) "If I want to improve my closing ratio by decreasing the numbers, I need to improve the precision of my prospecting." That sounds good. But sharpening your selling scalpel is just as hard as making the steep numbers.

Companies and individuals invest enormous amounts of time and money in sales training, only to be frustrated when core habits and behaviors don't improve. That's because we all have settled into a comfort zone we don't want to leave, thank you very much. Our inner idiots stand guard at the door. Before we feign anger or disappointment with our inner idiots, we need to confess how much we enable them.

One of our inner idiots' favorite excuses is, "I didn't know what to do." Pleading ignorance is great—except that we know damn good and well that we do know what to do. We just resist doing it, at all costs. The idiot inside all of us sits through sales seminar after sales seminar: arms folded, chin dropping to chest, dozing off, bored to sleep. If our inner idiots were honest with us, they would come right out and say, "Wake me up when they get to the secret of making the simple easy." Sleep on, idiot. It's not going to happen.

In case you're wondering how powerful your inner idiot is, how often do you fail to follow what you know to be the best course of action? How often do you embark on the best course of action only to wander off course, never to return? If it's that difficult for you to act in your own best interest, what makes you think your customers are any more skilled at it? *By recognizing, accepting, and getting better acquainted with your inner idiot, you will better understand and appreciate the inner idiot that's blocking your customer from buying.*

We added the emphasis to that last point because it's that important. As a sales professional, you have far more in common with your prospective and existing customers than you realize. Everyone has an inner idiot acting to sabotage the right choices. The more skilled you can become at managing your inner idiot, the better equipped you'll be to disarm the inner idiot that's blocking your customer from buying.

There is no end to the clever ways inner idiots (ours or our customers') devise to derail our best intentions. Sitting by the pool or playing golf until our inner idiots run out of ammunition won't work. We try, nonetheless, because waiting for things to improve on their own is a great excuse for personal inertia. It's not a great excuse, actually. But it's a common excuse. Do you want to be common or uncommon? Your inner idiot is perfectly happy with common. Here's a question to keep you awake at night: "When you allow your inner idiot to determine your behavior, what does that make the outside you?"

News flash from a successful person to his or her inner idiot: "Buckle your seatbelt, we're choosing in. Get over it. Simple is only easy in the small stuff that doesn't amount to much. We're going to amount to a lot. Trust me. You'll love it once we get there."

PREPARATION AND PASSION

Everybody claims that he or she wants to win. Ergo, we never ask people if they *want* to win, have more, earn more, or live more fulfilling and rewarding lives. Here's a list of more appropriate questions:

- Can you live with losing—not having what you want?
- Can you live your life achieving less than you deserve—living less?
- Can you tolerate mediocrity?

If you don't have all that you want, the answer to these questions is, "Yes." Truthfully, how many people really have everything they want? Let's not get silly here. Having what you want is relative. Do you want to live in reality or in some mystical haze?

None of this is to say that we can't, or shouldn't, want more than we have. Unless you are the rare and exceptionally mature adult who has learned to fully appreciate all that you have, there are probably a few things you'd still like to get your hands on. Passion for more in life is a good thing, as long as it can be broken down into realistic, doable actions. The bottom line here is that each one of us is capable of thinking and doing bigger and better than we're thinking and doing at present. So, passion and a desire for more should be on our radar screens.

Are you willing to admit that your willingness to accept less indicates a lack of the passion required to live a life of choice and win consistently? In other words, your inner idiot is winning more battles than he or she should be winning in an ideal world. You can always perform up to a low level of expectation. As you prepare for enthusiasm about success in selling, and in life, you will need to tolerate not having all that you truly desire. But don't confuse tolerance with acceptance. Don't be so impatient that you're not willing to put up with the limitations that accompany personal and professional growth.

Neither should you be so patient that you allow the flame in your personal pilot light to flicker out.

You must pump yourself up before you'll ever be able to pump up your *i*-customers. Your *i*-customers will respond more to how you feel about yourself and your attitude than they will respond to your product, your price, or your pitch. In other words, you can't fake it. Even an idiot can pretend to be excited. Even if you *can* fake it and get away with it now and then, you can't fake it forever and hope to get where you want to go. If you try and operate under false enthusiasm, you'll always wind up starting over again, having to squirrel up new customers.

Start by showing more enthusiasm for what you do. Enthusiasm is like a magnet. Your infectious enthusiasm will infect more customers in your life when you're more enthusiastic yourself. Your enthusiasm is like an insurance policy to your customers, idiots or not. When they see and believe that you like what you do they'll have more confidence that you'll actually act in their best interest.

If you can't get excited about your job every day, or keep yourself motivated, you may be in the wrong line of work. Start getting more excited about what you do—or find something else you can get excited about and do that. If you're insincere or disingenuous you'll be fair game for your customer's inner idiot, and your pitch will be eaten alive. Enthusiasm is one of the little things that add up and give you the edge you'll need to win over your toughest customers. Don't be so eager to rush into battle before you put on your game face.

PREPARATION AND PRODUCT KNOWLEDGE

In winning over your *i*-customers, product knowledge is paramount. Product knowledge creates credibility and confidence, and helps close deals. Your *i*-customers will not even begin to listen to someone who doesn't have a firm grasp, not only of their product or service, but of what it will do to solve their problems, make them feel 6 inches taller, 10 pounds lighter, and/or make them more attractive to the opposite sex without chemical enhancement. Part of the reputation and credibility you build for yourself comes from knowing your product inside and out; product knowledge increases your self-confidence and the confidence your customers have in you.

Certainty in solutions comes from product knowledge. The certainty in your sales presentation is also enhanced by product knowledge. Your *i*-customers will pay more attention when they sense that you know your stuff. The second they smell a rat, however, you don't know what you are talking about, your battleship is sunk. This isn't a call to fake it, although great salespeople have the ability to think on their feet. The ability to think quickly on your feet is enhanced by knowing every feature and benefit, in and out, and nut and bolt, about what you're selling.

You must look and sound like the expert. Heaven forbid if your prospective customers perceive that they know more about your product than you do. If so, "bye-bye." Game over. You lose. There is nothing more insufferable than an inner idiot who has the upper hand. Do your homework, but don't forget your finesse. In doing your homework, you might wind up knowing more about your customers' businesses than they do. Even if that's the case, don't come across that way. That would embarrass the person with the ink to sign your contract.

To earn more you must be willing to learn more—about your product, and about yourself. You can't afford to become complacent about your continuing education. Complacency about learning creates indifference, and indifference to learning opens a window of opportunity for your competition. Learning more about your product or complacent indifference are choices; your choices. Product knowledge is another little skill that, when perfected, will add to your ability to win over *i*-customers. Product knowledge is like doing slam dunks on six-foot basketball rims. If you miss, something else is seriously wrong.

PREPARATION AND THE WRITTEN PLAN

One reason that many salespeople are so successful at becoming average is that they don't have a written business plan. You can't expect great results unless you have a great plan, in writing. A written plan doesn't need to be perfect. But there is magic in writing your intentions down. The act of writing tends to ground your psychedelic hallucinations. It helps you order your thoughts. It helps you prepare your pitch.

Even idiot customers can sense when you don't have a plan and are just winging it. Without a plan, you make it easy for your customers' inner idiots to knock you off-balance. If you're not mentally, spiritually, emotionally, and physically prepared, *i*-customers are likely to knock your legs out from under you every chance they get. With a written plan you won't just get lucky more often, you'll deserve to get lucky. Sometimes you'll win over your *i*-customers only because you're well prepared; they simply needed to encounter someone with his or her ducks in a row.

Your pitch doesn't need to be perfect to win over your *i*-customers—or any other customers—as much as it needs to be honest and passionate. Having a written game plan laid out for yourself gives you solid footing and an organized agenda, which anchors your passion in confidence. Your plan should define what winning means to you. What is the perfect outcome for a sales call? (Hint to your inner idiot: it should end with your potential customers asking, "Where do I sign?")

Don't be surprised when you get the order. Expect to get it. With a written plan it will be much easier to review what is and isn't working. You can make adjustments as you go. Too many salespeople keep doing what isn't working. If you're digging holes in the wrong place, digging them deeper won't help. Without a written plan, how can you track results and make adjustments? How can you determine a better spot to dig? Thinking that you're saving time by not writing down your plan can indefinitely postpone winning over your prospective customer.

PLANNING IS NOT PROCRASTINATION

For too many sales professionals planning becomes synonymous with procrastination. Spending weeks, months, or years working on your plan is called delay of game. As long as you're planning you have permission not to get out there and work, right? Wrong. No matter how brilliant your plan is, it won't produce sales. Selling produces sales, and there is only one place selling takes place—in front of a current or prospective customer. Oh sure, planning is safe. When planning, there are no rejections, no objections to overcome, and no sales. While you're busy planning, someone might dial your number by mistake and buy something. Realistically, though, you might as well be singing about *running across the valley beneath the sacred mountain.*

The next 12-step program might be called Overplanners Anonymous. "I'm Bill. I'm an overplanner." Are you always on the verge of action? Do you believe in the concept of "ready–fire–aim?" You're much better off to get out there, find out what's working and not working, then call a timeout and make quick adjustments. Don't paralyze yourself by overplanning.

PREPARATION AND MOTIVATION

If you're not motivated to sell, what makes you think your customers will be motivated to buy? Go back to the passion discussion and consider what motivates you. Money? Freedom? Independence? Acknowledgment and recognition? Be sure you're clear about what keeps you going, and why. Remembering and understanding why you are doing anything can provide all the motivation you need to keep going. When you forget why, you begin to lose steam without realizing it. When the *why* is clear you will do whatever it takes to produce the results you want. It's tough to remember why you're doing something when you're in the process of losing or being rejected.

If the customer is truly a clueless creature, yet has nevertheless managed to get your eyes off the prize, you weren't sufficiently aware of your core motivations. Write these things down. Revisit them daily. Recite them periodically. Chant them like a mantra. Keep the things that motivate you fresh in your mind. Include your strong and wonderful qualities. Using positive reinforcement to pump yourself up is not the time to be modest. Don't count on your *i*-customers or your boss to tell you these things. It's not their job. (Well, it is your boss's job.) But do you want to hitch your wagon to his or her success? Eventually the buck stops with you. You might as well take responsibility now.

The why you're doing something is more important to a positive outcome than the what, the how, or the when. Make sure your why is big enough. Write down why you're in sales. If what you wrote doesn't get you excited, it won't provide the motivation to get you through the tough days or win over your toughest customers. Keep writing. Your truest motivations may not be among the first few things you write. When you hit it you'll know. Your palms may begin sweating. If nothing you write about why you are in sales excites you, write about what excites you and figure out if a sales career is the best way to get there. Your *i*-customers might not be able to see the why in your eyes, but they will be able to ascertain whether or not you have one.

PREPARATION AND PERSONALITY

Not every current or prospective customer is an idiot and not every idiot is a current or prospective customer. As we mentioned at the beginning of this chapter, a customer's desire, need, or the appropriateness for the goods and/or services you're selling, his or her ability to pay, and an awareness of how much he or she will benefit from the purchase are all factors in a customer's decision to buy or not to buy. However, treating customers like clueless creatures, even when they are, is risky business. There are many personalities you'll need to deal with in the course of your sales career. Some are more pleasant than others. Some are more difficult to deal with than others. Some you won't want to deal with at all. But as many successful sales professionals will tell you, the toughest customers are often the ones who buy the most and the most often.

Connecting the dots between your essential motivations and customers' buying habits will help you navigate these sometimes treacherous waters. Knowing a little about these personalities and what makes them tick will also help you get and keep their inner idiots between your crosshairs. Pay attention to what these people say and do. What magazines and books are in their offices? Are there pictures of their spouses and children around? Are there pictures of fish they've caught? In other words, do a little detective work so that you'll be able to know your best enemy. Prepare for these people.

Prepare for the Machiavellian

This character sees the world as a pyramid. There is one spot at the top and, in his or her mind, that spot belongs to the Machiavellian by divine right. The Machiavellian is no idiot in terms of cluelessness or ignorance. He or she is probably very strategic, calculating, and potentially dangerous. If you get in his or her way, he or she can reach down your throat, pull out your heart, and slap it in the palm of your hand while it's still beating. Don't worry, it's nothing personal. You merely got between the Machiavellian and the top spot. It could have happened to anyone—and it will, if he or she wanders into the Machiavellian's path.

Your best approach to a Machiavellian personality is to recognize and accept his or her obsession with power. Your best message is, "What I'm selling will help you acquire the power you deserve and hold on to it." It's best to make friends with Machiavellians, especially if you're selling business-to-business. If the Machiavellian is any good at all he or she is likely to reach that top spot, become the big kahuna, and wipe out anyone who threatens his or her lofty domain. If your choice is to have a Machiavellian as a friend or an enemy, choose friend.

Prepare for the Sadist

Unlike the Machiavellian, who maims and destroys only as a means to an end, the sadist kills for sport. Sadists seek powerful positions because they can wreak more havoc and cause more suffering from positions of power. If you're selling business-to-business you'll notice the sadist getting off on the weeping and wailing coming from the cubicles. The gnashing of teeth and rending of garments is a sheer turn-on for a sadist in the workplace.

Never challenge the sadist's power. Your best behavior in the presence of a sadist is wincing. Whatever you do make it appear painful. Don't miss opportunities to compliment the sadist on how hard he or she is making his or her employees work. In your case, as you make it appear that the sadist is causing you immense discomfort, be sure to acknowledge how the sadist's cruel and unusual demands on you will make you a better person.

Prepare for the Masochist

Whereas sadists get off on causing pain to others, masochists bring pain upon themselves whenever possible. We should say: They bring pain upon themselves like clockwork. Masochists visualize their lives as colossal disasters and want to enroll you and anyone else in those disasters at their earliest opportunity. If you work for one, you're not in a career-enhancing environment. Masochists are not bad people. They just want you to experience what they experience, which is right neighborly of them, if your neighbors hate you.

As a normal human being you want to rescue masochists from their pits of despair. It's difficult to accept and remain aware that they prefer it down there. Selling to them is, therefore, tricky. While you don't want to go over the top and promise them that the products and/or services you're offering will cause them pain and anguish, you can't exactly paint a picture of a bright and rosy future, either. With masochists, you need to play it by ear and make sure they understand that, while the goods and/or services you're selling will do what you claim they'll do, the results won't be so marvelous as to take away *all* of the masochist's problems.

Prepare for the Paranoid

To paranoid persons, especially in the workplace, everything anyone does is part of a grand conspiracy against them. If so accused, don't try to deny it. Don't claim to be leading the grand conspiracy. That's a little too over the top. Perhaps you can just admit that you've heard talk. But don't claim to be part of the underground. Whatever has caused the paranoid person to suspect you (or most anyone else for that matter) has nothing to do with you. At least we hope it doesn't. Your duty to maneuver around and/or through the paranoid's maze is a responsibility you have first and foremost to yourself.

If you feel up to it, you can promise your current or prospective paranoid customers the names, dates, and places involving their imaginary conspirators, should they come to your attention. We're not seriously suggesting you play mind games. But we do highly recommend against intimating that your potential or existing customers are crazy, even when they appear to be. Just remember that paranoids don't get much sleep, so maintain control in their presence. Don't make any loud noises or sudden moves if you can avoid it.

Prepare for the Greek God or Goddess

We use Greek gods and goddesses as our example because if an organization is large enough, there is room for polytheism. There can be as many gods as there are people who are anxious to self-deify. Zeus, Neptune, Apollo, Athena . . . these people usually just have a bad case of primary narcissism, but you need to play it right. "I don't know anybody who plays god," you say incredulously. Oh, yeah? What do you think Donald Trump is doing on *The Apprentice*? He sits on a throne of judgment with operatives seated at his right and left hand. People come before his throne of judgment and plead for their jobs as he sits serenely with the symbolic power of life or death to dispense as he wishes. Nice gig, if you can get it.

You probably sell to a few small-*g* gods. When you enter their holy of holies (offices or homes) do you bring tithes and offerings? Burn incense? Bow before them? It probably feels a bit sacrilegious to humor them in such a way. But the big-*G* God must roll with laughter at these clowns. The problem is, if you roll with laughter—no sale. Try and keep a straight face as you convince them that what you're selling will glorify their majesty. Get their name on the contract and get out before they lose their temper and send a swarm of locusts over to your house. It could be worse. They could say, "You're fired."

Prepare for Your Best Buddy

There are people who are looking for companionship. Anybody will do. If you walk through the door at the wrong time, it will be you. Like any of the wacky personalities you'll deal with from time to time, you need to be prepared for your best friend. If you're not prepared you'll be joined at the hip and it will require surgery to separate yourself. Your medical insurance provider will no doubt consider such surgery cosmetic and/or elective, so you'll have to pay for it out of your pocket. It pays to pay attention when we tell you to prepare.

Knowing what you know and having had the experiences you've had with emotionally needy people, there are lots of clues available for how to close them. We're not suggesting that you exploit their neediness or anybody else's psychological eccentricities. Being prepared is a matter of not being blindsided as you present your case in a language that everyone will understand, based on their unique psychological eccentricities. Your new buddy will want to come to your house for Thanksgiving, to watch the Super Bowl, and even have a sleepover with your kids if you let him or her bring those jammies with the feet on them. Ignore uniqueness in others at your own peril.

Prepare for the Decent Soul

Thankfully, most people are decent and reasonable folks. They have a pretty well-balanced concept of what's right and wrong and can distinguish between needs and wants. At the end of the day they're a lot like you. Their inner idiots play the same games on them that your inner idiot plays on you. You have so much in common with regular people that understanding their wants, needs, and intentions should be a piece of cake.

Decent Souls are, of course, subject to blocking your sales in the same way you're capable of blocking someone's attempt to sell you. Your best move is to be your usual genuine, authentic self, and let your enthusiasm for your products and/or services shine through. People who are most like you will be the quickest to recognize and respond to your honesty and authenticity.

CHAPTER ONE SUMMARY

When we say be prepared or be the idiot, we're serious. As a sales professional, cluelessness will cost you big time. Your cluelessness will cause you to miss opportunities. Your customers' cluelessness will comfort them as they refuse what you're trying to sell them. Either way, cluelessness is your enemy. The inner idiots, yours and your customers', will derail your selling agenda faster than a speeding locomotive. Or is that a speeding bullet? Either way, you're screwed. Your best hedge against getting hit by a speeding locomotive and/or bullet is to be prepared to sell.

- Pro-intentionally sell to prospects, not suspects: it's about need and intent. More often than not, you swim in the same water as your customers. You traverse the same (or very similar) intersections of needs and intentions. Your goal is to find a way for your needs to intersect with your potential customer's intentions or vice versa.

- Choose in: Being prepared and making career expansion and enhancement priorities in your life requires intentional and deliberate action on your part. Your success won't happen by accident. Wishing and wishing and wishing won't do it. You must decide to do the things you know need to be done. You must make that decision daily, or even more frequently if that's what it takes to stay on track.

- Don't confuse simple with easy: The road to riches appears simple and straightforward. Indeed it is. But actually following those steps, one after another, day in and day out, is hard. Knowing what to do is easy. Consistently doing those things is hard; especially the consistency part. Just look back over your life with 20/20 hindsight and ask yourself, "Which or how many ships would have come in if I had stuck with the program over time instead of getting impatient and moving on?" The time passed anyway, didn't it?

- Passion and product knowledge are the fuel that keeps the boiler hot: The written plan keeps your locomotive on track. You don't want your inner idiot driving when you get up a good head of steam. That's a recipe for a train wreck. Of course, if your inner idiot is too involved your planning process will turn to procrastination, and you'll never get a head of steam up at all—much less go anywhere. Knock your inner idiot out of the box by concentrating on what it is you want in life. As you focus on what motivates you your boiler should start heating up all on its own.

- The multiple personality issue: All kidding aside, different people march to different drummers. Sometimes, *very* different drummers. In sales you must deal with the Machiavellians, sadists, masochists, paranoids, buddies, and decent folks. The well-prepared sales professional will stand a much better chance of succeeding than someone who is taken by surprise and off-guard by people who seem to lie awake at night figuring out how to take sales professionals by surprise and off-guard.

Be prepared. If you were a Boy or Girl Scout, you have that covered. We just helped you fill in the blanks and sand off the rough edges. There is so much at stake in your professional sales career that preparation has never been more critical to your success. In Chapter Two we'll build on preparation by learning more about communication skills—or as we prefer to say, "Connecting with the Clueless."

2

STEP TWO: CONNECT WITH THE CLUELESS

Idiot customers don't know the finer points of connecting and communicating, so it's up to you to make the connection and to ensure that communication takes place. Once again, the customer's shortcomings are your opportunities. Regardless of where your opportunities come from or what form they take, seizing the opportunity and working it to your advantage will prove to your inner idiot that you're in charge. An idiot encounter can provide you with lots of information about the idiot before he or she realizes you're gathering information at all—if he or she ever realizes you're gathering information.

That was part of your genius plan, right? You're out to learn as much about your prospect as possible, as fast as possible. Being a great communicator begins with being a fast learner. Great communicators use what they learn to connect with idiots—or anyone else, for that matter—in meaningful, productive, and profitable ways.

This is a language-learning step, and there's a lot of language to learn. Like everyone else, idiots are never not communicating. Their body language is just as information-packed, sometimes more so than others who possess a greater awareness of the world around them. People with keen self-knowledge, (as in how the rest of the world perceives them), can be very cagey about what kind of image they put forth. They are also keenly aware of the possibility that you're working them. When it comes to idiots and their clueless natures, what you see is what you get. They'll expose just about anything for the world to see and they probably don't have a clue when you're working them. We'll wager that the last time you got worked over by an expert your inner idiot was at the controls.

Studying idiots is the fastest way to connect in a way that will profit you. What is the idiot's energy level? What is he or she most curious about? How does he or she perceive you? Friend or foe? In other words, does your *i*-customer open up when you show up or does he or she become defensive and shut down? How does he or she feel you perceive him or her? Is your *i*-customer bold and confident in your presence or does he or she duck and cower when you reach into your briefcase?

If customers don't buy you, they'll never buy what you're selling. Whether or not prospective customers are comfortable with the product you're offering them is irrelevant unless they are comfortable with you. At the end of the day there's not much difference between a genius who doesn't buy and an idiot who doesn't buy, except for your pride. Allowing your current or prospective customers to buy your competition's products, or worse—to buy what you're selling from someone else—should be punishable by law. Caning wouldn't be a bad punitive technique for sales managers to employ on lethargic and/or insincere salespeople—except for the fact that so many sales managers deserve to be caned for the same things.

IDIOTSPEAK

Let the one who is a perfect communicator cast the first stone. That will keep the rocks on the ground. Ever since *How to Work for an Idiot: Survive and Thrive without Killing your Boss* was released (Career Press, 2003) businesspeople have been studying their bosses' mannerisms, behaviors, thoughts, desires, and language. All of the verbal and nonverbal signals are part of his or her idiotspeak. Every one of your current and prospective customers has his or her own form of idiotspeak. Because each of us has an inner idiot we can at some level speak idiot. But, different idiots have different dialects.

So it is with your existing and prospective *i*-customers. Idiotspeak is all around. Pay attention to how your customers decorate their homes, offices, or shops. Are there lots of family pictures on the wall? Sports memorabilia? Stuffed animals? Mounted fish? Miniature guillotines? What types of magazines and/or newspapers are lying around? *Are* there magazines and/or newspapers lying around? What kinds of books are present? What subjects does your customer insist on discussing that have nothing to do with what you're selling?

Get the picture? By never not communicating, we're all communicating all the time, in a hundred different ways. Wardrobe, grooming, shoes, accessories. . . . The condition of wardrobe, grooming, shoes, and accessories. . . . All of it tells part of the tale. Everybody has a story and you need to learn your prospective customer's story if you intend to become part of it. That's what happens when you become a trusted supplier of your *i*-customer's needs and desires—you become part of his or her life. That won't happen unless you can speak his or her language.

No matter how sincere, honest, and authentic you are as a person and as a professional (and we hope you're exceptionally sincere, honest, and authentic), how is your customer (*i* or otherwise) supposed to be comfortable with you if you can't speak his or her language? It's not your *i*-customers' job to learn your language. It's your responsibility to learn theirs. How else can they possibly feel at ease around you? How will you be able to make all the necessary assurances to ensure your prospective customers that they'll be happy after they make the decision to buy from you? You must learn idiotspeak and speak it fluently.

YOUR STORY

There are three sales to be made in every sales call: you, your product, and your company—in that order. For all the reasons we've already mentioned, you are the first sale you need to make. If you don't sell your *i*-customers on you, how can you sell them on the other two? A big part of helping your prospective customers feel comfortable and confident with you, and thereby make you part of their lives, is to share your life with them.

You must give *i*-customers a good reason to choose you. You must create a compelling story about you and what makes you different from other salespeople. Focusing strictly on your product, price, or company won't do it. You'll get to product, price, and your company soon enough if you first sell what's wonderful about you. What's unique about you? We often hear salespeople talk about their Unique Selling Proposition (USP). We think that should be changed to your Unique *Self* Proposition.

As with your products, services, and company, if you don't believe in yourself, your *i*-customers won't believe in you either. If you don't believe in yourself, you might be able to fool an *i*-customer some of the time. But, a genius customer will never be fooled, and nobody will be fooled forever. Believing in yourself is about self-esteem. If your self-esteem is in short supply you know what you need to work on first if you expect to ever make a good living at selling.

Self-esteem is a function of self-confidence. Self-confidence is a function of attitude. Ultimately, attitude is a function of the preparation we mentioned in Chapter One, along with the confidence that comes with it. Thus, self-esteem, attitude, and the confidence that comes from preparation are all part of your story. More specifically, issues like self-esteem, attitude, and the confidence that comes from preparation form a backdrop upon which your life is projected for your customers to see.

The aspects of your life that you want to share with your current or prospective customers, idiot or genius, need to resonate with their lives. Why would your customers or anyone else want to think of you as part of their lives if everything about you creates dissonance with them? "What am I supposed to share with them about me?" you ask. That's easy. Take your cues from your customers. Become the good detective we referred to earlier. Study them. Become a passionate listener and an ardent observer.

You might not be a hockey fan. However, if your *i*-customer has a hockey stick propped up in a corner of the office, uses a puck for a paperweight, has a Wayne Gretsky screen saver on the PC, wears a New Jersey Devils jersey to work, and is missing at least one front tooth, you can bet your bottom dollar she's a hockey fan. You don't need to become an expert about hockey to dazzle her with your conversation. In fact, if you try to be a hockey expert, you're likely to come off as phony and insincere. That blows the honest, genuine, and authentic thing.

The best way to remain honest, genuine, and authentic, even when discussing hockey, is to use what you know—or learn just enough to ask intelligent questions. Just because people love to talk about themselves doesn't mean they don't need a little encouragement now and then. A skilled salesperson knows how to prompt an existing or prospective customer to talk about the things the customer loves. First of all, observe and gather data about what interests your customers. Then give them every opportunity to talk about their interests, even if it includes a little cuing. All the while you weave your story into their story.

YOUR *I*-CUSTOMER'S STORY

People love to talk about themselves, and they like to be listened to while they talk about themselves. Get to know them. Be a good listener. Make eye contact. Learn when to lean in and when to lean out. When the talker is heading toward the direction you want, lean in. If he or she is vectoring off the path of greatest profit to you, lean out. Either way, remain interested, *really* interested, in what they have to say.

Show your *i*-customers you are truly listening by using their names—often. Ask conversation-opening questions. Don't be thinking of what you are going to say next while they're talking. Ask clarifying questions. Show them that what they have to say is important by repeating what they say back to them. By asking the right questions you will learn a lot in a short time. Everything adds up to shape and define the relationship that emerges between you and your *i*-customers before any selling takes place. As they're speaking your radar is sweeping. With every comment they are communicating more about who they are and what they want.

WHO VERSUS WHAT

You connect with people at the level of *who* versus *what*. The amount of time you spend connecting and building relationships will depend largely on the personality style of your customers. Some people like social connection first and business second. Other personality styles prefer business first and social second. Some prefer business and nothing but business.

Size up your prospective customer's style quickly. If you sense that you're dealing with a business-first type don't spend a lot of time talking about the weather or if he or she likes playing golf. There is little margin for error here. A business-only customer is most concerned with what you have to sell and how it will benefit his or her business interests. If you get too chummy, you may be told, "I have enough friends. If you have something that will help me be more successful, lose weight while I sleep, make my spouse and/or any other significant idiot in my life more physically attractive and/or attentive, I want to hear about it. Otherwise, next."

If your prospective customer leans back from you when you speak, if his or her pupils narrow to pinpoints, you're working from the wrong script for his or her type. If his or her pupils dilate, it's steak and lobster tonight. If you are just shooting the breeze with the business-first customer, he or she will resent you for wasting his or her time. If you go right to selling with the person who wants to take the time to get to know you first, he or she will assume you don't care. With relationship-driven people no relationship means no sale. They want to have a strong sense of who you are before any purchasing takes place.

If the first question out of your prospective customer's mouth is, "What's the price?" don't be an idiot and start telling him or her all about your trip to Maui. He or she doesn't want to hear about it, at least not until you've disclosed how much what you're selling is going to cost. The key here is to adjust your presentation style to match his or her personality type. Note that we said, "Change your presentation style to match his or her personality type." You can't change your personality type to match his or her personality style.

PERSONALITY IS JOB ONE

Although we maintain that every man, woman, and child on the planet has an inner idiot, not every idiot is a customer—and not every customer is a complete idiot. In Chapter One we introduced you to a variety of customer types, all of which you'll encounter as you sell business-to-business or business-to-consumer. Psychologically speaking, you can't change your personality type the way you can change your socks. A chameleon can change colors to blend into its surroundings, but it's still a chameleon. So it is with you. You can use enhanced listening skills to determine which personality types you're dealing with and reflect back to them that part of their personalities that will make them most comfortable with you and what you're selling.

There's nothing wrong with making other people comfortable; especially *i*-customers. You're not tricking them, nor deceiving them. You're merely exercising good social etiquette. How many women would be thrilled if their husbands or boyfriends reflected back to them the aspects of their own personalities that make them feel most comfortable? How many men would do handsprings to be in a relationship where their significant other reflected back to them the aspects of their personalities that make them the most comfortable?

How many bosses would be eternally grateful if their team members hung on every word they said and did everything they wanted them to do? How many team members would like the same thing from their bosses? Why should you feel the least bit guilty or manipulative for being a good listener and making your existing and prospective customers feel comfortable? Certainly you have an ulterior motive. Who doesn't? Do you think a significant other is going to go out of his or her way to make his or her significant other feel comfortable without an agenda attached? Sorry to burst your balloon. Life is what it is; all of us scurrying around trying to get our needs met. People are people and fairytales don't come true without the cooperation and contributions of others.

Connect with the Machiavellian

Connecting with a Machiavellian is easy, although it may not be something you're necessarily proud of. Perhaps the easiest way to make your presence known to a Machiavellian is to impede his or her progress toward the top of life's ladder. Sure, you'll wind up staring down at a handful of beating heart, but you'll know that you got his or her attention, at least for as long as it took for him or her to remove you from his or her path. As we mentioned before, simple doesn't equate to easy and, likewise, easy doesn't necessarily equate to smart.

The smartest way to sell to a Machiavellian is to connect in a way that will make him or her aware of how you are toiling to advance his or her career aspirations. That begins with learning what those aspirations are. Back to the detective work, the anthropological research, and learning Machiavellian-speak. Without being too transparent, make it clear that you believe he or she would move the organization forward much faster than the current administration. In consumer sales, make it clear that whatever you're selling will provide the lifestyle, comforts, and/or status that he or she rightfully deserves.

Connect with the Sadist

Whereas the Machiavellian hurts other people only as a means to an end, to the sadist, hurting people is the end in itself. Connecting to a sadist for the purpose of selling something is a touchy proposition. You certainly don't want to get into the habit of hurting people—at least we hope you don't. So then how can you best connect with a sadist without becoming one yourself? Understand that a sadist can't operate without power. Self-respecting sadists don't run around picking on people who are bigger than they are. Attacking people who are capable of attacking back takes all of the fun out of it for sadists.

You might have guessed already that sadists tend to be bullies. It's not hard for 800-pound gorillas to beat up on 400-pound, 200-pound, and 100-pound gorillas. Taking on another 800-pound gorilla doesn't interest them. So don't try to connect as their equals. Don't volunteer to be their punching bag, either. Without being too maniacal about it, make sure your comments acknowledge how powerful they are. Let them know how what you're selling will increase and expand their power and thereby increase their ability to wreak havoc on those around them. You might want to leave that last part unspoken, but nonetheless implied. If you help a sadist feel more powerful he or she will connect the rest of the dots.

Connect with the Masochist

Turn the sadist inside out and you have the masochist. The poor babies can't do anything worthwhile even if their lives depend on it. When you encounter walking, talking colossal failures it's natural to try pumping them up with a pep talk. Wrong move. Masochists don't want to feel better about themselves. To them, being positive and affirming feels as unnatural as you would feel purposefully dropping an anvil on your toe. Connecting successfully with masochists is a matter of keeping them in their comfort zones or misery. Same difference.

We don't suggest you clobber them with caustic comments despite how much they might appreciate such treatment. What you can do is let masochists know that what you're selling won't solve all the problems they're facing in life, which is probably true in any case. Masochists don't necessarily want to drag others down to their levels, although that happens when others try to reinflate a deflated masochist. Mention that what you're selling will make life easier, more pleasant, and even productive for others around the masochist, and the masochist might just buy into an effort to prove he or she is the only one worth loathing.

Connect with the Paranoid

Connecting with paranoid personalities hasn't become any easier since Chapter One. It's still a dicey proposition. Paranoid people are still, well, paranoid. Everything you do will be considered part of some grand conspiracy to undermine them. The best way to connect is to make them feel as though you sympathize with their paranoia. Not that you're a believer in conspiracy theories yourself, but you might be convinced that such things exist.

Being an active listener comes in handy with paranoid personalities. The more you listen and focus in on them, the more they might believe that you're interested in their stories. Paranoid people like to tell stories about conspiracies and the conspirators plotting against them. They must feel that you're safe to talk to first. That's a plus for you, because unless they feel safe there's no way they're going to buy from you.

Connect with the Greek God or Goddess

Some of your *i*-customers might truly believe they are Neptune, Zeus, Apollo, Athena, or Donald Trump. No matter. Connecting with them is merely a matter of honoring their delusions about themselves. A gentle bow when you enter their presence, cast your eyes downward until spoken to. Offer your hand to them tentatively, don't thrust it toward them. The last thing you want a small-*g* god to think is, "Who does this person think he or she is? Doesn't he or she know how to act in the presence of a living god? Perhaps a thunder-bolt or two will get his or her attention."

Connecting with a small-*g* god is a great place to unload all the swag piled up in your office. Small-*g* gods don't usually get snippy over the quality of the merchandise, as long as you don't show up at the holy of holies empty-handed. A coffee mug filled with Hershey's Kisses and wrapped in cellophane is usually enough to get you in the door. If you've done your corporate anthropological study and found golf paraphernalia around your *g*-customer's office or home, a dozen new Nike balls will bring a smile to any golf-god's face. Of course a dozen Nike golf balls might put you in debt for a couple of months. So you must decide the relative value of buying your way into the Greek god's or goddess's favor.

Connect with Your Best Buddy

Most sales professionals spend an infinite amount of time and energy getting in to see prospective customers. When the customer wants to be your best friend the sales professional winds up counting the minutes until he or she can leave. Connecting with buddy cus-tomers is easy. Getting them to buy is something else altogether. If they think that signing the contract will mean you'll leave they will put it off as long as possible with delay tactics.

When you suggest looking over the contract and/or catalogue, be sure to add, "There are a zillion things to choose from in here and you're going to have lots and lots of questions, so let's get started." The promise of going over every detail of the products you're selling is tantamount to reading your *b*-customer bedtime stories. Mention that if he or she signs this contract you'll be back soon with new and improved ones.

Connect with the Decent Soul

As we mentioned in Chapter One, decent, hard-working souls don't appreciate being cajoled or manipulated. They just want the facts and nothing but the facts. That actually makes your life pretty easy, unless the facts don't support what you're selling. Whether they do or they don't, connecting with a decent soul is as simple as telling the truth, plain and simple. A frank, honest, and open discussion with a decent soul is refreshing.

If you're having trouble convincing people that they'll be happy with their decision to buy what you're selling, there must be something wrong with what you're selling, or your pitch, or both. If you're selling the best goods and/or services that money can buy, for a reasonable price, the decent soul will likely buy. If he or she continues to balk, think of the words penned by Elbert Hubbard (*The ERA Magazine*, March 1916):

"I try to fix my thoughts on the good that is in every soul and make my appeal to that. And the plan is a wise one, judged by the results. It secures for you loyal helpers, worthy friends, gets the work done, aids digestion, and tends to sleep o' nights. I will influence men, if I can, but only by aiding them." A good approach then. A good approach now—and one that will be appreciated by decent souls everywhere.

COMPONENTS OF CONNECTION

It's always good to have a toolbox full of communication tools. That way you can choose the right one to fit the circumstances. Powerfully select the words you use. How you say things can be more important than what you say. Be energetic. Utilize body language in getting your point across. Spoken or unspoken, language is language. Research at UCLA has proven that when communicating to another person or getting your point across,[1] seven percent of your successful communication is attributed to the words you speak, the tone in your voice accounts for 38 percent, and your body language makes up the other 55 percent. Don't be an idiot and put all your effort into the words you choose, ignoring the other 93 percent of your message. In the final analysis, communication has very little to do with the words coming out of your mouth.

[1]Mehrabian, A., & Ferris, S. R. (1967). Inference of attitudes from nonverbal communication in two channels. *Journal of Consulting Psychology, 31*, 248–252.

If you feel clueless with your customer, you may need to stop putting so much credence in what you have to say. In other words, stop waxing so eloquently with your mouth when some body English will go a lot further. Eye contact is powerful, as is mirroring the posture of your prospective customer. When your *i*-customer is expressing deep and abiding concerns about something—from business, to family, to the cat's sniffles—only an *i*-salesperson would sit without a furrowed brow, on the verge of tears.

A NEW SKILL CALLED CONNECTING

Nobody demonstrates this better than kids. Kids naturally learn about using verbal tone and body language as part of their communication strategies. Remember when you learned how to ride a bicycle? You probably began with training wheels. Eventually, for a time, when the training wheels were removed, things became more difficult and precarious. You struggled to stay upright, maybe even falling a few times and scraping a knee, an elbow, or both. As you practiced, it's likely that one of your parents walked beside you, giving instructions, encouraging you, and catching you if you lost your balance. You were scared, but excited. You looked forward to the time when you would succeed; when you would at last ride free and on your own. So you kept at it every day, and eventually mastered the skill of riding a bike.

You never asked if you would learn to ride. You were merely impatient to reach the time when you would ride on your own. So it is with the development of new skills, such as connecting and communicating in a productive manner. Do you move forward with excitement, willing to perform unsuccessfully until you master the challenge? Do you jump at the chance to try something new or to prove yourself in the face of unforeseen obstacles? If you're like most people who outgrew their Peter Pan suit long ago, the answer is probably, "No."

What's changed between your bike riding days and today? For one thing, we'll bet you've become a lot more concerned about the opinions of others, often hesitating because of possible criticism or ridicule. Sure, it can be uncomfortable to try something new, perhaps even scary. But if you take your eye off of the prize and focus your attention instead on how others may view you, you're asking for failure. You need to return to the confidence you felt when "if" was not a question. When it becomes strictly a matter of "when," you're not only riding that bike, you're flying along with no hands.

THE GREAT BALANCING ACT

By learning how to balance two basic agendas—the need to close the deal and the need to develop relationships—every salesperson can become a star performer. Great salespeople are able to apply both talents equally. The salesperson who focuses too much on relationship building will make a lot of friends, but few sales. The salesperson who is too preoccupied with closing the sale will forfeit a great deal of customer loyalty and repeat or referral business. Nevertheless, despite all that we've shared with you so far, there are folks who still don't get it. They invoke too much "who" when they're dealing with a "what" customer, and vice versa.

What causes salespeople to get off balance and lose their connections? Why do some salespeople get stuck in the relationship mode, while others get obsessed with closing at the risk of alienating their best prospects? We believe it could be as simple as addictive behavior patterns. The first casualty of being addicted to anything is often balance. Life becomes so skewed to the needs of the addiction that everything else takes a back seat and the person's life tilts in one direction—most often the direction of getting one's immediate needs met (i.e., a fix).

In sales, that tilt may be more subtle, but no less damaging. Sales professionals can lose their professional edge if they fail to balance their talent of forming relationships with their need to close sales. Any activity with a good measure of gratification associated with it can have the prospective of becoming addictive. It doesn't matter if it's drinking, gambling, shopping, spending money, running, or working in sales. While other professions usually offer highs for people only when they reach the very pinnacle, in selling, anyone can get a rush out of making more sales.

Does closing a sale give you a high? Do you get excited every time you meet a new prospect? People in sales can easily become addicted (thrown off balance) by the adrenaline rush associated with certain phases of the sales cycle. Is there anything wrong with pumping your fist through the air and expressing a triumphant "Yes!" when you get the contract signed? Not in our book; as long as you are able to maintain balance. If you really enjoy selling, and if you don't get hung up on any one particular aspect of it, such as meeting new people or closing, you're not likely to suffer from an addictive pattern.

TAKERS VERSUS EXCHANGERS

The closing-addicted closers are attractive, intelligent, witty, and often financially successful. They are focused on numbers and obsessed with sales goals and collecting commission checks. Their main preoccupation is to sell something to everyone they meet, at any cost, whether they ever meet that person again. They want to get their fix and then to quickly move on to the next prospect. Closing addicts say they like people, but they're only using people to satisfy their impulse for a temporary high.

Closing addicts are often takers instead of exchangers. They take what they can from everyone. Closing addicts rarely talk about their personal lives and usually don't have time for small talk. They wear a polite yet unemotional mask. Closing addicts tend to feel their self-worth is tied to closing sales, which is why they tend to feel more vulnerable and take it more personally than others when they do not or cannot close a sale.

Closing addicts are usually not good team players, since they have a hard time giving up control. Sales managers generally like closing addicts for one reason: They get results. However, their high sales often come with a high price—cancelled sales and lost referral business.

The relationship addict, of course, also presents some unique and potentially harmful behaviors that can drive sales managers crazy. Many relationship-driven people pursue a career in selling because they like to meet other people. New relationships often carry the promise of new sales, a better future, and the potential of dreams come true. Although there is nothing wrong with feeling good about connecting with new prospects, some salespeople become so gratified on an emotional level that they actually avoid closing the sale. To relationship addicts, fresh new prospects are always a source of excitement. When new prospects appear, relationship addicts can't wait to get their relationship rush.

While they're on a roll with personal relationships they feel powerful and worthwhile. But at the same time, they feel ill at ease with advancing the sale. They worry about spoiling the warm, comfortable feelings when they finally move from the relationship component of sales to discussing business. Relationship addicts are, metaphorically speaking, intoxicated on the relationship. To them, other parts of the sales process don't offer an equal amount of gratification.

CHAPTER TWO SUMMARY

Optimum sales results come from getting connected and staying balanced. You are in front of the prospect for two reasons: (1) you are interested in the person, his or her wants and needs, and (2) you want to make the sale. Both are valid. Both are important. Here are some keys to connecting and maintaining balance:

- Make a connection: Learn to read and interpret your prospect's signals. More than that, learn your *i*-customer's language. Some call it Idiotspeak. Know how to communicate with your current and prospective customers and know how to interpret the signals they give you. When the relationship goes well, advance the sale. When the sale goes well, move on to the close. But stay connected throughout.
- Know who you're dealing with: By studying the type of personality with which you're interacting, you can find resonance much sooner and often avoid disengagement and dissonance on their part. Connect with the prospect on a personal level: Smile, show emotion, and listen to the customer's wants, hopes, and dreams. Engender trust and confidence in yourself and your company. Be firm: Have the inner desire to close the sale. Firmness is the ability to confidently lead the conversation from personal matters to the business at hand and direct the sales process from the opening to the close.
- Strive for balance: While friendliness opens doors, firmness closes sales. To achieve success, you must balance both

qualities. How? Develop a plan for connecting with your existing and prospective customers. Build both a solid relationship
with your prospect and a sales strategy for closing the sale.
Apply the concept of balance to managing yourself. Strive to be
firm and friendly with yourself. Firmness helps you set more
challenging goals, but friendliness will help you enjoy the rewards.

- Your story/their story: It's ultimately about the story. The
sooner and more authentically you can become part of their
story, the closer you are to closing—again and again. Learn the
background to your *i*-customer's story. In fact, find those
places where your inner idiot shares common ground and mutual concerns with your customer's inner idiot. Inner idiots
converge at that great (although hidden) crossroads of success.

- Be an exchanger, not a taker: Closing addicts tend to be takers,
and as a result they rarely see customers more than one or two
times. Most selling careers are enhanced by strong relationships that are built over time and that last a long time. Don't act
like an addict in search of a fix. Your current and prospective
customers, idiots or geniuses alike, will feel used and abused,
and very likely will be. That's not good for you, for them, or for
your company. Learn to honor and enjoy every stage of the
sales cycle.

We've discussed connecting and communicating with customers,
idiots or not. Now it's time to move on to some advanced applications of communication technique: Confusing and Clarifying. The
ability to skillfully confuse and clarify is to basic communication
skills what riding a unicycle is to riding a bicycle.

3

STEP THREE: CONFUSE TO CLARIFY

The Detective Colombo approach to selling is loaded with questions, designed to both confuse and clarify. Confusion is a powerful sales technique, especially when you're holding virtually every information card. But even then only when masterfully applied. It's not hard to confuse the clueless. The beauty is that you can clear up the confusion on cue. You choose when to clarify the water or when to make everything clear as mud. Timing as well as critical information is under your control. The questions you ask and the answers you provide set the pace.

The more straightlaced and starched-collar crowd calls this "editorial prerogative" or "information management." Even if you prefer to call it the "judicious dissemination of data on a need-to-know basis," it's meant to organize your prospective or existing customer's thinking around the purchase of whatever it is you're selling. It's your job to organize your *i*-customers' thinking to the best of your ability. It's not an easy job. Part of what makes customers idiots is the fact that they're unschooled in how to buy. Worse yet, they're unprepared to listen.

Isn't that the same idiocy we're all vulnerable to? You might have been studying how to sell for your entire adult life and still have no clue about how to buy. It's often said that good salespeople are the most illogical buyers around. Whether that's true of you, when customers don't buy no one sends them to a seminar to learn how. Sales professionals like you spend endless hours in the classroom, online, and reading books to learn how to sell. Every time you make contact with prospective or existing customers you're taking them to school, so to speak, and they're doing the same for you.

CONFUSION AS A TOOL

Confusion plays several roles in learning. How many multiple-choice tests have you taken in your life? The point wasn't necessarily to confuse you as much as to demonstrate your ability to select the correct answer out of the midst of confusion. Selecting the correct answer from the multiple incorrect answers is clarifying. As young students ourselves we felt that selecting the correct answer out of the midst of multiple incorrect answers was usually a matter of luck. Nevertheless, it felt good to be lucky. If your *i*-customers are feeling confused you have the opportunity to make them experience that same good feeling of laser-sharp clarity.

This is particularly true of late-afternoon sales presentations. Everyone is an idiot by 3:30 in the afternoon. Creating confusion won't be a problem. Clarifying the confusion, however, will be practically impossible. Your customer's mental operating system will already be shutting down and in serious need of defragging. Therefore, don't equate being unreasonable with being an idiot. You might be calling on someone who has passed the point of diminishing returns.

Realistically speaking, you probably don't need to intentionally confuse your prospective customers. They are plenty confused before you arrive. Even though people are often reluctant to admit they're confused, you nonetheless need to acknowledge it and perhaps even remind them of it. Mention that you understand how difficult it is to make decisions about how to address the personal or professional problems facing them. Your customers always have a lot of choices available, and every choice creates a different scenario. Depending upon what you're selling, you always want you and your product to be part of the final scenario.

In all likelihood your *i*-customer could very well be saying to him- or herself, "This idiot salesperson is right. Although I'll never admit it, I am confused by all the choices available to me. That's why I usually do nothing. Not making a decision is making a decision, right? So, that's my decision." When you see your customer's eyes glaze over you know he or she has drifted into that abyss-like internal conversation, and might never come out. That's your cue.

SURGICAL QUESTIONS

Never prescribe the medication before the diagnosis is complete. Questions are surgical and strategic tools to elicit the critical information you need to determine what's going to make your *i*-customers feel good about buying from you. Who knows that better than your inner idiot? If you wouldn't buy why should they? The whole process of discovering the customer's wants, needs, desires, wishes, and so forth, starts with listening. Listening, like well-crafted questioning, is a double-sided scalpel. It's important that your prospects feel listened to. But they should never know how much you're really hearing.

Asking open-ended questions about the issues you've already determined are important to your current or prospective customer—hockey, for example—will give him or her an opportunity to express his or her innermost feelings. He or she might not be aware that you're making mental notes about those feelings. He or she might think that statements about the fight with the spouse that morning, how adolescents and employees never listen, and how all the other sales professionals in the world annoy him or her are just throwaway comments. But not you. You're busy weaving an intricate tapestry out of all the threads you learn about this current or prospective *i*-customer.

"So, paying 40 percent more on your utility bills is not your definition of cost cutting?" you inquire. If the answer is the predictable "No," you've significantly narrowed the range of conversation. You've also clarified something that, believe it or not, might not have been as obvious to your *i*-customer as it is to every other carbon-based life form on the planet. "Are you saying that you want more sales for every advertising dollar you spend?" Duh.

Every question, rhetorical as it may be, gets at least one thing clear, and everything you can clear up helps direct the conversation down the path to your company's door. As you improve your detective and anthropology skills, just walking into someone's office or home can unleash an avalanche of clues as to what he or she wants. If there's a picture of a pimple-faced kid in a graduation cap and gown on the desk or mantel you can reasonably assume the proud parent would like to see his or her son or daughter successfully reach the next milestone in life. What do you have in your bag for that?

THE RIGHT QUESTIONS TRUMP THE RIGHT ANSWERS

The right questions promote possibility thinking; opening up the possibility that your current or prospective customers will buy. Top salespeople have the ability to ask great questions. They don't merely offer their *i*-customers the answer that they think might solve the problem. Most clueless salespersons spend more time coming up with clever answers than they do in perfecting their questions. No matter how brilliant *i*-salespeople think they are, or how earth-shattering the answers they offer their current or prospective customers, said customers are much more highly motivated to buy if they feel the answer (i.e., buying from you) is their idea.

The correct strategy is to lead your customers to the water. By the time they get there, providing you're a talented salesperson, it won't just be a pool of water—it will be a cool pool of water in the midst of a scorching desert. Really great sales professionals go way past the cool pool in the scorching desert thing and lead their customers all the way to the Promised Land (i.e., buying from you). Your *i*-customers will follow your questions like crumbs through the forest.

It's colossally narcissistic for an *i*-salesperson to assume that his or her pitch is such a thing of beauty that the customer simply can't wait to hear it. Some *i*-salespeople are so in love with themselves and the answers they bring to their potential customers that they get annoyed when customers interrupt them. Some *i*-salespeople believe that their entertaining presentation can overcome anyone's bad day or argument with a spouse or mother-in-law (including arguments with the spouse caused by the mother-in-law).

Some *i*-salespeople must be gently reminded that they aren't bearing the answers to world peace or a cure for cancer. Some need to be *brutally* reminded that they aren't bearing the answers to world peace or a cure for cancer. It's a photocopier, for heaven's sake. Or a water softener. Or supplemental life insurance. Sales professionals need to allow *i*-customers to discover what they want, need, and desire—with some subtle guidance from the *i*-salesperson, of course.

If you simply give the answer to your customers, they won't have a journey to make. It will all seem too easy. Whenever it seems too obvious, easy customers invariably start to wonder, "What's the catch?" By blurting out the answers to their problems, you've robbed your customers of any sense of adventure and discovery. It's not your discovery they care about—it's their own. Even colossally ignorant customers know that any answer you offer is biased. If they think they've discovered the answers themselves, they'll trust the answers more than they trust you.

They could be convinced to trust you if you have the time to invest. With long-term customers, if you've treated them fairly and responsibly, there probably will be a certain level of trust built up over time. However, it's a much more practical and expeditious approach to lead customers to their own conclusions and help them find their own answers in the magic bag of goods and/or services you tote around. Of course, you don't want the answer they discover to include buying from somebody else.

So, polish your question skills. Ill-advised questions can lead your *i*-customers down the wrong path, to the wrong conclusion and the wrong behavior. You don't want them to feel as good about buying from somebody else as you've made them feel about buying from you. That means you need to be a better tour guide than your competition. You need to make your customers more comfortable and secure buying from you, none of which is helped by flapping your gums incessantly.

The right questions generally make the *i*-customer feel as if he or she is part of the conversation. More than just a part of the conversation, truly skilled questions give your *i*-customer the distinct impression that he or she is running the conversation. The right questions, verily, the great questions, create quality dialog. Your questions, although soliciting information, are directing your *i*-customer's reasoning in the direction you want it to go and keeping it between the navigational beacons of your choosing.

The right questions will allow you to show off your listening skills. The person across from you in the office, over the kitchen table, on the other end of the phone, or answering your email will get a sense that you're listening by the fact that you're not interrupting them. A more powerful and surgically precise tool is reflecting information back to him or her, therefore not misinterpreting. If you can articulate thoughts and ideas formulated in his or her head, he or she knows you're not in there, ergo you must be listening. If you're listening, you care. If you care, she or he feels good. *Capiche?*

No one ever developed a grudge against someone who listened and paid attention too well. How many motivational speakers have reminded you that two ears and one mouth should be used in that ratio? It has been said so much that most states have passed laws prohibiting motivational speakers from saying it any more. Senate bill 276-89—"We got it already." If we do the math correctly, the forbidden reminder reveals that every answer should be twice as long as the question, minimum. That means a long-winded, closed-ended question that elicits a "yes" or "no" answer should be punishable by no less than five years hard labor in the sales gulag.

Compelling questions reveal your *i*-customer's wants, needs, and desires. Any sales professional who thinks he or she has all the answers isn't asking the right questions. Being a poor questioner can also be a sign of underpreparation on the part of the salesperson. The more research you conduct on your current and potential customers, the more leading and effective your questions will be. The more you know about your customer's wants, needs, and desires before you cross his or her threshold, the more compelling your questions will be.

SET THE STAGE AND PLAY THE PART

It sometimes pays to appear a little confused by what your *i*-customer says. Confusion can go a long way toward clarifying needs. The more confused you look the more details your *i*-customer will reveal and the more targeted your next question can be. The illusion of confusion can be healthy. Look how well Detective Colombo did with the illusion of confusion when he already knew the killer's identity. As long as you don't overplay it and come off like an imbecile it can work well for you, too. Use questions that evoke your *i*-customer's motivation to buy, such as questions that begin with "Why?" "Why is that important to you?" or, "Why is that a concern?"

Even if you understand your customers' needs, asking them to expand on their responses is another opportunity to connect and to keep them engaged in the conversation. Ask questions like, "Can you tell me a little more about that?" "It sounds like that is important to you, am I right?" This is another opportunity to demonstrate to the customer that you're listening. Be sure and take copious notes, pausing only to gaze thoughtfully into your *i*-customer's eyes or furrow your brow—whichever you think will draw out more information.

Remember that withholding information, especially pertinent information, is your *i*-customers' job if they are trying to be cagey, which is usually the case. Most of the time they won't reveal the real issues of importance to them; it's your job as a salesperson to ferret those out. Keep asking, stay confused, be curious, and force your *i*-customer to clear it up; on your cue, of course. Ask your *i*-customer, "Am I on the right track? Is this close to what you're looking for?" Stay on offense, not defense, but don't begin selling until you're certain what your potential customer's challenge or problem is, and you're confident that what you're selling can solve it. If you aren't sure, ask more questions. Only your commitment to stay in the question longer than is comfortable will provide you the information you need to move on.

FROM THE MOUTHS OF BABES

Kids have no problem being confused, curious, and clarifying in situations when it's in their best interest. It seems like all of their questions begin with who, what, when, where, why, and how. Remember, your *i*-customers will never be sent to buying school because they don't purchase what you're selling. Not buying comes naturally. Neither are kids sent off to a special school that teaches them how to illuminate a conversation. It comes naturally. They have an innate ability to discover other people's hot buttons, especially in adults. It's all a game to them. Maybe you're taking it too seriously, or stopping too soon with your current and potential customers, which could also be something you need to unlearn. Over time, you may have learned so many answers that you forgot the questions. When the question becomes more important than the answer real growth will occur.

Kids are great little Socratic (questioning) machines. They figure that if you could only see the situation the way they see the situation you would agree to let them have their way in a heartbeat. To that end they keep it up, with relentless questions. They will create wildly imaginative, hypothetical situations until you are compelled to agree. "What if space aliens were about to destroy the earth unless you let all children eat ice cream before dinner? I mean, just imagine for a moment if it actually went that far," the child reasons, with complete seriousness and sincerity. "The earth is hanging in the balance. Would it really matter anymore when kids ate their ice cream? Even though the possibility of this happening for real is remote, do you want to take that chance?"

If you want your current or prospective customers to see the world the way you see it—like kids do—then creative and strategic questioning is the way to go. However, nobody likes getting talked out of his or her worldview. That's where skilled questioning will come in handy—to help you capture a vision of the world through your customers' eyes. That's where their reality is. That's also where their comfort zones can be found. Great questions can convince others that you've joined them in their world.

PERSONALITY-BASED QUESTIONS

Have you noticed a pattern? In each chapter we remind you that one size does not fit all. There are a wide variety of personalities you must deal with while earning a living as a sales professional. Not everyone will respond the same way to the same questions. Confusion will look different on different people. Here is our list of the usual outrageous personalities.

Ask the Machiavellian

Your questions should reinforce what the Machiavellian considers his or her divine right to the top spot. For example, instead of asking,

"What do you feel is the biggest threat to your organization?" ask, "What is the biggest obstacle between you and the advancement you deserve?" The Machiavellian definitely has an answer to that question. He or she might be too politically savvy to expose his or her hit list to an outsider like you. But, if you manage to earn the Machiavellian's trust over time, you're likely to get a good chunk of business. You earn that trust, of course, by convincing the Machiavellian, through your consistent actions, that you're solidly in his or her corner, and a champion for his or her career ambitions.

Ask the Sadist

This one gets a little more squirrelly. The Machiavellian is looking to move up, and doesn't hesitate to cause pain and suffering to others in that quest. The sadist just wants to cause pain and suffering, whether he or she moves up or not. We recommend you stay with the power angle mentioned in previous chapters vis-à-vis the sadist. Sadists can only hurt those people over whom they have institutional power. Instead of asking, "What do you feel is the biggest threat to your organization?" ask, "What do you think will enhance your power and influence within this organization?" What he or she does with that power is none of your business, right? Of course, he or she won't be interested in anything you have to sell unless it will enhance his or her power and influence in the organization, so you know how to prepare for the pitch.

Ask the Masochist

Masochists place themselves in a peculiar position that can work to your advantage. While they want nothing to do with anything that would make them feel good, they might not object to people around them feeling good. After all, if you want to feel miserable what could be better than being surrounded by happy people? It's like rubbing salt in your own wounds. Now, that's what masochists dream of. Instead of asking a masochist, "What do you feel is the biggest threat to your organization?" ask, "What do you think will make the people closest to you, the people you come into contact with every day—truly happy?"

Ask the Paranoid

It's against the paranoid person's essential nature to trust you or anybody else. You could, given enough time, possibly convince your paranoid customers that you're not out to harm them. But, retirement, yours or theirs, might get there first. The shortcut to success with a paranoid person is similar to that of the Machiavellian, the sadist, and the masochist. Use their personality disorders to your advantage. Instead of asking a paranoid person, "What do you feel is the biggest threat to your organization?" ask, "Who do you think is behind the problems you face, and how can I help you counter the threat they pose?"

Ask the Greek God or Goddess

Talk about a high opinion of oneself. Anyone who thinks he or she is in the same league as The Donald is scary to behold. Nevertheless, they're out there, and you must deal with them sooner or later. We've already coached you to burn incense and bring tithes and offerings when entering their holy of holies. Despite the melodrama, what's the worst that can happen? They can fire you, right? Or not buy from you, which is essentially the same thing. Instead of asking a small-*g* god, "What do you feel is the biggest threat to your organization?" ask, "What can I provide to you that will be a blessing and proper tribute to your sovereign leadership? If nothing pops into your head, I have a few suggestions."

Ask Your Best Buddy

With friends like this, who needs family members? Questions are no problem with your best buddy. He or she wants to talk all day, and all evening, to you. Don't give your best buddy customer your home phone number. A question like, "What do you feel is the biggest threat to your organization?" will only prompt more discussion about the next fun outing together. Your best buddy doesn't care about threats to the organization. You'll get a lot more mileage from asking, "What can I do to get you off my back?" Just kidding. Try, "What can I provide that will help you help others and make lots of new friends in the process?"

Ask the Decent Soul

There are people who really care about doing whatever it is they do and serving whomever they serve. If they're businesspeople they will likely be on the lookout for ways to provide better service to their *i*-customers, or to build a better mousetrap. If it's a consumer sale you're dealing with, they are likely to be most concerned for the health and well-being of family members or significant others. Instead of asking, "What do you feel is the biggest threat to your organization (or family)?" ask, well—come to think of it—you might as well ask, "What do you feel is the biggest threat to your organization?" After all, the decent soul will actually care.

BIG SUCCESS COMES FROM SMALL STEPS

Most people are casual about not having what they say they want. They actually rationalize that it's okay to settle for less. Most people are great successes at becoming average. Nobody reading a book titled *How to Sell to an Idiot* wants to be average. The first step to getting what you want is to stop settling for less. Raise your expectations and you might be amazed at what you can achieve if you're prepared to invest enough blood, sweat, and tears. Skills such as confusion and clarifying must be framed within a larger sense of success.

Success and achievement begin with making a choice. Learning and applying these skills is the right choice for your future. People who have what they want have made more right decisions than wrong decisions in critical areas. It makes no difference if it's in business, athletics, relationships, or in school. Those who make a conscious decision to win, more often than not, do. They know what they want and they back it up with sustainable action until they get it. The key words, in case you didn't notice, are "sustainable action." Curiosity is the genius of all sales and clarifying questions are curiosity in action.

To make the year ahead your best ever you must be willing to do things you've never done before. Ask questions you've never asked before. Clarify confusion as you've never clarified it before. You'll need to improve, really improve. To get more you must be and do more. It is going to take more than positive thinking. There are plenty of positive thinkers with empty bank accounts. Before you run out and spend your last dollar on self-improvement books, tapes, and CDs, remember that self-improvement books, tapes, and CDs don't change people—action changes people.

If you are really ready to go all the way and make the year ahead your best ever, here are five areas that you must master lest the next 12 months look like the previous 12. We're not proposing a radical change. You just need to find a way to get a little bit better, bit by bit, day by day. It's called incremental improvement. Five percent improvement in five areas of your business will yield a 25 percent increase in your overall effectiveness. You only need a slight edge to win consistently.

Critical Area One: Clarity of Purpose

Most people fail to reach their goals because they don't have a big enough purpose—no vision for their business. You must have a big *why*. Start by answering, with certainty, the question, "Why am I doing this?" The purpose of your business is the *why* that will keep you motivated during rough times, the bad days, your darkest hours. Without the *why* being clear, bad days turn into bad weeks. Bad weeks produce stress and cranky people. Stress increases blood pressure. High blood pressure stiffens the walls of your heart.

You don't need a cardiac event. Rather than focusing only on the consequences of confusion in purpose, focus instead on the good things that can come from clarity of purpose. The *why* leads to fulfillment. Without fulfillment, you can't achieve total success. Begin by revisiting why you're in the business you're in. Make sure it motivates you, or you may be wasting your time—and setting yourself up for health problems to boot.

Critical Area Two: Written Plan of Action

Every great outcome starts with a great plan. Knowing what you want is the first step. Knowing when you want it is the second step. As we mentioned before, writing it down is what gives it life. To consistently hit your targets you must know what they are. In our experience less than 15 percent of all loan originators have a written business plan. That's insane. What's the percentage of folks with a written plan in your business or industry? Probably not much better. Writing down goals and plans to achieve those goals creates a demand on performance. Most of us don't like demands; even those we put on ourselves.

Your written plan must address who your customers are and how you will find them. Your plan must also account for the obstacles you will hit along the way and how you will overcome them. By anticipating obstacles just like you anticipate customers you won't be so surprised when they show up. Also, address your core motivation and how you will stay motivated to go all the way. It's difficult to play full out without a clear intention of where you are trying to go. Write down your plan and get on with it. For help writing down specific and measurable action plans, see *The Art of Constructive Confrontation* (Wiley, 2005).

Critical Area Three: Participate

Intention without action is some people's definition of insanity. It's everybody's recipe for inertia. It takes more than good looks and good ideas to succeed. (If you can only manage one, have good ideas.) Only action will close the gap between what you have and what you want. Goal setting that includes more wishing and less working won't work. Even so, there is no magical correlation between the number of hours you work and the success you achieve. We meet hardworking salespeople all the time who have little to show for their efforts. That's why working smarter makes so much sense.

Using the techniques in this book and keeping your sense of humor handy will make the work you do pay bigger dividends. Get smart. Use your strengths every day. Life is too short to perfect your weaknesses. Get out there and show up earlier every day, stay later, and bring more of yourself to the game. It has also been our experience that you can eliminate 50 percent of your competition just by working more diligently. Most people want to put in a little effort and win the big prize. There is no shortcut to success. To win a lot you must show up a lot. You never know when you might get lucky. But, what's the use of luck if you're not there when it happens along?

Critical Area Four: Track and Review

Question and clarify yourself. Don't wait until the fourth quarter to see if your plan is working. It may be too late to make any meaningful corrections. Track your activities and review your results on a daily basis. Be sure you aren't falling back into your old, bad habits. Note what kind of results you are getting for the amount of time, energy, and dollars you're investing. Develop some kind of tracking form that will make it easy to see if you're getting closer to or further away from your targets. Without tracking your activities and reviewing your results regularly you'll find yourself working too hard for too little results.

Critical Area Five: Make Adjustments Swiftly

Most successful people failed in their struggle to the top. They saw what wasn't working and made the necessary adjustments along the way. Failure also helps you find the edge of your capabilities. Don't be too attached to your plan. It's either working or not. If it isn't working, make adjustments. There is magic in finding the right place and the right time. Actually, there is no magic involved. You merely need to keep searching. If you find that you're looking in the wrong places go look somewhere else. If you are digging holes in the wrong place, digging them deeper won't help.

If you proceed with clarity of purpose, a written plan of action, if you track and review and make adjustments swiftly, you can maximize your chances when the intangibles take over. It is your moment—don't miss it. You truly can go all the way by committing to get a little bit better every day. "Yeah, yeah," you might be mumbling, "Motivational gobbledygook." It's gobbledygook if you don't do anything with it. If you light your afterburners and put the gobbledygook into action it becomes money in the bank. Remember your purpose.

CHAPTER THREE SUMMARY

Confusion comes naturally. Sometimes you need to help it along a little to create a cloud that only you can clear away. Customers, even *i*-customers, won't buy amidst confusion. Only an *i*-salesperson will try to *sell* in the midst of confusion. Customers will buy when they have a sense of clarity. The truly great salespeople realize the benefits of confounding their customers to a point and then presenting themselves as great clarifiers. Questions are the most surgically precise clarifying instruments in the hands of a master sales professional.

- Take a cue from kids: Accept that curiosity is the genius of all sales and that great salespeople ask great questions. Great questions reveal the customer's real needs and asking clarifying questions can actually help clarify the customer's desire.
- Questions connect with your customer: By using your eyes and ears more than your mouth and your visual aids, how your customers respond to your brilliant questions will draw a road map right to their bank accounts. Listening is one of the most endearing and effective qualities in communication. You'll know you're getting closer to your customer's needs when the customer is doing most of the talking. Never stop looking and listening for clues.
- Seek self-clarity: One surefire way to know that you didn't connect with the customer is leaving without a sale and being confused as to why you didn't get it. That's characteristic of an *i*-salesperson in action. To make matters worse, an *i*-salesperson will leave without a sale, not have a clue as to why the customer didn't fall all over him- or herself in response to the *i*-salesperson's fabulous answers, and go back to the office to tell the sales manager that the customer is an idiot.
- Questions by any other name: Relative to the vast importance of listening there is comparatively little sales training available on the subject of listening, connecting with your customer, and using curiosity to help define your customers' needs. At best, most sales models use the term "probing." Isn't that what dentists do? Probing can cause confusion, but not as precisely as skilled questioning.
- Decisions are made out of clarity: Decisions are postponed out of confusion. You might want to intentionally postpone your current or prospective customer's buying decision until he or

she proves ready to buy your product. Masterfully transform confusion into clarity so you can present solutions that make sense to your customer. Confuse to clarify. The clarity you create will make your customers comfortable enough to buy from you.

Now that you've spent some time dealing with preparation, connecting, and confusing to clarify, it's time to move on to matching up what you have to offer with what your current or potential customers want and need. We call it the Match Game, because having the right sales professional, the right product, and the right company to best fill your *i*-customer's gap won't mean anything until you match them up.

4

Step Four: Play the Match Game

Many sales professionals fail to recognize that the would-be idiots across the desk from them think $2 + 2 = 5$. Therefore, when the idiot salesperson speaks in a $2 + 2 = 4$ language the customer never gets comfortable enough to buy, and the *i*-sales professional can't figure out why. On the other hand, some sales professionals are clever enough to realize that their customers believe $2 + 2 = 5$. Unfortunately, the *i*-salesperson's typical response is to teach the customer a new language instead of learning the customer's language and translating accordingly.

Clarity can be achieved either way. But current and prospective customers might not want to learn a new language. Conversely, we've never met a customer (idiot or otherwise) who objected to our learning his or her language. In fact, the latter is the hands-down favorite in our experience. In the end, the prospect's perceptions must match your proposed solution or your proposed solution must match your current or prospective customer's perspective. Take your pick. If not, there will be no comfort achieved—and no sale closed.

Matching your *i*-customer's problem with your solution is as much a matter of semantics and situational reality as anything else.

Your solution is probably a legitimate $2 + 2 = 4$. But you might need to present it as a $2 + 2 = 5$ in order for the customer to feel comfortable about it. Selling can be a game of mixing and matching. A skilled sales professional will present trial closes to test the waters and to see how miscalibrated the customer's perception is. What does the potential buyer respond to: benefits, values, or emotions? Each trial match moves your *i*-customer closer to buying and moves you further away from idiocy.

PUT IT IN REVERSE

The steps to winning over your toughest customers that we've covered so far are:

- Be Prepared or Be the Idiot
- Connect with the Clueless
- Confuse to Clarify

In case you're starting to feel overwhelmed by the thought of wacky sales calls filled with goofy, quirky, elements, this is all very practical stuff. We'll expand on these and other elements as the book progresses. For now, understand that a sales call is basically won or lost in 2 minutes. You actually will go through a complete cycle in four 30-second quarters.

The First 30 Seconds

Demonstrate that you're a reasonable person, because every contact is predisposed to hate the fact that you're intruding on his or her precious time. The very first question you need to answer is one your prospective customer will never ask you in so many words. "Why should I listen to you?" is what he or she might say if he or she were to be completely honest. Actually, you might have heard that question asked—if not in those exact words—in language that wasn't too difficult to translate. "Mr. Smith," you say preemptively. "I wanted to sit down with you today because (fill in the blank)." Straight to the point.

Why are you there? If you fill in the blank with "... because you are the only thing between me and my commission," you're wasting everybody's time. If you hand him a patronizing handful of cow chips you might as well have said "... because you are the only thing between me and my commission," for all the good it will do you. You're there because you are a reasonable human being and you understand how important it is to focus the precious little time you have on products and solutions that will help Mr. Smith breathe easier, walk a little lighter, and sleep a little more soundly. You have 30 seconds to make your intentions clear, thus proving that you're a reasonable person.

The Second 30 Seconds

Set the table. Set three tables, actually. Now that you've convinced Mr. Smith that you're not there to shoot the breeze, become his new best friend, or rob him blind, tell him what's about to happen. "On this table," you say, motioning to an area on his desk, "is the situation you're dealing with." You can put a name on that if your preparation has been sufficient to not insult him by demonstrating how much you don't know about his business or personal needs.

Motion to the second area on his desk and say, "On this table is the solution that (my product) can provide. On this third table," you continue, "is the way we're going to make that happen. But, before we get more into what's on these three tables, I want to give you a quick overview of who I am." Now, you're ready to move into the third quarter. You've now demonstrated that you're a reasonable person, respectful of Mr. Smith's time, and have an intelligent grasp on his situation.

The Third 30 Seconds

Now you name the three most impressive credentials you can about your company and your product. The company is a concept. What you're selling is a commodity. The concept and the commodity must be complementary. You immediately relate how proud you are to represent a firm with that kind of track record and reputation in the business community. The implication is clear that all of this integrity can be brought to bear on Mr. Smith's issues. He should appreciate such an implication. If you are sufficiently articulate he'll begin feeling increasingly comfortable with you and the company you represent.

If you haven't distilled the essential qualities of the company you represent and the ways that you reflect and embody those essential qualities you're not ready to be out selling. In some places it's called an elevator speech. It's quick, but it's not dirty. In fact, it's quick and clean. No ambiguity. Speak in headlines. The unspoken but clear message Mr. Smith should receive is, "Me and my company . . . we're players."

The Fourth 30 Seconds

Close. You heard right. Close. It's said that if a statement is true you don't need many words to embellish it. Be brief and to the point. Mr. Smith has heard your eloquently prepared lead-in. So, close him already. If more professional salespeople attempted to close in the first 2 minutes of a pitch their closing ratio would go up. More often than not, the longer a presentation drags on the greater the opportunity for the *i*-customer to disengage. The longer you talk about what you're selling the more likely your current or prospective customer won't buy it. Don't talk yourself out of a sale.

Close by painting a word picture for Mr. Smith about what the future looks like after he buys from you. "Let me tell you what I hope will happen here today," you begin. Be creative, be funny, be engaging, but be prophetic. Make the picture something vivid and real so that Mr. Smith won't have to stretch his calcified and long-dormant imagination very far to believe it's possible.

BRING IT HOME

From the first words out of your mouth to the closing in 2 minutes. You've got to be good. No need to confuse to clarify or sweat what kind of personality you're dealing with. Here's why I'm here, here's what I have for you, here's who you're working with, and here's what can happen. Those 2 minutes might be enough for Mr. Smith to buy. Having said that, we're perfectly aware that it might not be enough. But you laid out a case and established credibility.

Mr. Smith might say, "That's all very good, but let's shoot the breeze for a while." Now you know what he wants from you. Amusement? Perhaps. More information about you and your company?

Perhaps. Companionship on a lonely afternoon? Possible, but not probable. All of the above? Maybe. Let your *i*-customer tell you when it's time to reach into your bag of tricks. Don't assume you know best. That's what your inner idiot would do.

The better prepared you are and the more detective work and anthropological study you've performed on Mr. Smith and his organization, the better. But after you've completed your first 2 minutes he'll take you where he wants to go. This is where leading and following become one. You must demonstrate in your demeanor and your delivery a deep and abiding respect for Mr. Smith. Well, at least abiding. If you only see him as an idiot standing between you and your commission, you're not going to be tuned in to take advantage of what he wants and needs.

Your ability to empathize with Mr. Smith's situation—and convey that empathy—will determine your success. Mr. Smith is about to fill in the blanks for you regarding where he is experiencing pain. You must be paying attention through active listening. If you're busy formulating an answer for Mr. Smith you'll probably miss the answer he's handing you on a silver platter. At the end of the day (just as it was at the beginning) selling is about compassion, not commissions.

The closer you are to feeling Mr. Smith's pain the closer you are to home. His pain might be caused by his inability to make a connection between what you're selling and feeling better. Just because you laid it out in an eloquent and concise manner doesn't mean he won't still be confused. Mr. Smith, after all, could be a complete idiot. Or he could be a sneaky little devil who is intentionally muddying the waters to test you. If you and your product can stand up to scrutiny, he reasons, he'll feel better about buying.

Either way, in the interest of bringing it home, doing a good job on the first three steps will make matching your product (solution) to your customers' wants and needs a piece of cake. If that sounds oversimplified, let's just say that a well-played match game will at least make the whole deal easier to swallow for everybody. If there's no sale after you do a good to fair job on the first three steps you'll at least have cake all over your face instead of egg. You'll also probably still be in the game instead of fouled out.

As we mentioned, use the information you've learned from your customers to find their hot buttons. Never stop gathering data. For instance, if you know that the most important thing for your customer is customer service, don't start off selling price. If your customers want blue, sell blue as if they can't live without it. Idiot salespeople will try and shove green down their blue customers' throats because the salesperson likes green best.

It's common sense to find out what customers want and give it to them. Yet, you'd be amazed at how many *i*-salespeople miss this basic concept by a mile. Then they'll tell their sales manager that their price is too high. When that happens your customer loses, your company loses, and you lose.

You need to get this match game thing right. There is no margin for error: There is no such thing as almost making the sale. The problem might harken back to the arrogance that we mentioned earlier on the part of salespeople. To an *i*-salesperson who thinks the world gets out of bed in the morning only to hear his or her magnificent pitch, it would sound reasonable (as unreasonable as it sounds) that the *i*-salesperson knows better what the *i*-customer wants than the *i*-customer. Sales professionals can't play the match game if their minds are already made up before they meet with their current or prospective customers.

The match game can spell life or death for the sale. Customers will ultimately buy from you because they believe that your product will solve their problem. Take charge and solve their problem, not yours. You may be required to bring out the big guns here, like your negotiation and listening skills. All of your preparation time will now pay off. You can use what you gained in preparation to begin negotiating solutions.

If you know your product inside and out, as we've talked about in Chapter One, and you can think on your feet, your customers will recognize you as the expert. Product knowledge is paramount. Can your product really do the job? This is where you come off as confident and certain or tentative and unsure. Attitude shows up as self-confidence—or the lack of it—as you match your solutions to your current or prospective customers' wants and needs. Remember that the level of confidence you have in yourself will be transferred to your customers and can assist them in making the correct buying decision. The correct buying decision is, of course, buying from you.

Matching Means More Selling, Less Telling

The match game is all about converting interest into action. Great salespeople not only have the ability to generate curiosity in their customers, they know how to transfer that curiosity into a closed sale. Zero in. This is the time for more selling and less telling. Don't waste time.

At the next opportunity to close the sale test the water. Go for a trial close. Ask, "Would you like to know the next step?" Then be quiet and listen to your customer's answer. If he or she says "No," that will be your first clue that you are off course or haven't provided the right solution yet. If he or she says "Yes," start writing, explaining the details as you go.

The word "yes" is definitely a strong indication that the customer is ready to buy. Don't be the kind of *i*-salesperson who hears "yes" and keeps talking. Some *i*-salespeople are so prepared to talk their customers into submission that getting a "yes" to a trial close throws their entire game off. For many sales professionals, especially those who are social animals, simply shutting up can be a gargantuan task. If your customer is hesitant but appears close to making a decision, questions will lead the horse to water faster than an avalanche of explanation covering everything you think he or she might be doubting.

THE NEXT STEP

Very often your customers are clueless as to what the next step is. They won't ever reveal that to you. They are probably unaware of the extent of their cluelessness. If you presume that everything that comes out of your *i*-customer's mouth is gospel truth, you could become an idiot about to become the victim of another idiot's cluelessness. In the end everyone is confused. When everyone's confused nobody buys.

Make it easy for your customer to say "Yes." Make it easy for the customer to buy from you. This is the time to fail forward. Risk a little and don't play it safe by waiting for your customer to start begging to purchase your product. You'll be safe—but sorry. Don't get us wrong—we'd all like that ego boost. Professional salespeople fantasize about customers begging to buy the way that pseudo-macho guys fantasize about playing football in the NFL. Guys who accept their physical limitations still fantasize about dating NFL cheerleaders. Many women fantasize about a "90 percent off" sale at Neiman Marcus or dating a guy with the physical prowess to play in the NFL. What would it be like to tell your sales manager that you don't have time to make calls because your voice mail is filled every morning with customers threatening to jump from the nearest overpass if you don't sell to them ASAP? Fantasies are just fantasies. You can't deposit them at the bank.

In the first 2 minutes you told your potential customer what you wanted to happen. If need be, grease that skid with a great question. No matter how eloquent you are, your *i*-customer may still have trouble tuning in to your frequency. "Tell me how you think this can help you" is a great question. It invites your current or prospective customer to paint a picture that will be to his or her liking. If not to his or her complete liking, at least it will be a picture he or she understands.

MORE LESSONS FROM CHILDREN

Kids have no problem floating trial closes. Kids learn to play it safe as they get older. Being willing to fail in the course of eventually getting what they want comes naturally to them while they're still young. Kids are also good at playing the match game, because again everything is a game to them. If a kid wants a bike, he or she might ask, "You want to see me learn to ride a bicycle, don't you?" The intent is to match your desire to see your kid learn to ride a bike with his or her desire for the bicycle. Some kids are so good they can match your desire for them to go to Harvard some day with buying a pony now.

As an adult, playing it safe will affect the kind of questions you'll be willing to ask. You may only be willing to ask questions that can only be answered with a yes. While that might make you feel safe, it won't get you closer to where you need to go. It may be time to unlearn how to play it safe. You can't get to second base without taking your foot off first base.

THE MATCH GAME AND PERSONALITIES

In the parade of personalities you deal with in professional sales the match game will mean different things to different people. The whole point of studying personalities is to better characterize and categorize what various people are likely to want. Your attempts to match the solutions your product offers to the wants and needs of your various current and prospective customers will be determined by how well you understand the basic human motivations that drive their thoughts and actions. A solution, no matter how brilliant, won't be worth a hill of beans to someone who is looking for something completely different.

A Machiavellian Match-Up

Your old friend the Machiavellian is looking for power. Not just power, but ultimate power. You have no idea if the Machiavellian will build an evil empire or be a benevolent dictatorship. The only thing you can take to the bank is that he or she wants to be in charge. Keep all of that in mind as you prepare to match what your product offers to the solution the Machiavellian is seeking.

As we said at the top of the chapter, it's a matter of perspective. Your perspective is not likely to bear any resemblance to the Machiavellian's. Whatever it is you're selling, if it leaves the door open to any possibility that the Machiavellian's agenda could be altered or blocked, you and your perspective are dead meat. The match you need to make before a Machiavellian will buy is directly between what you're selling, who you are, the company you represent, and his or her ascent to the summit. Do that and you're home free.

A Sadistic Match-Up

As usual, sadists are tricky to deal with, because your experience and motivations versus their experience and motivations are probably polar opposites. If you thrive on pain and suffering in others you don't need our advice. Your match with the sadist will be made before you walk in the door. Since that's not going to be the case 99.9 percent of the time, you'll need to be agile. Just throwing yourself on the floor of sadists' offices and writhing in pain won't do, because they know that they had nothing to do with your agony. That takes the fun out of it for them.

Your match game needs to appeal to the power the sadists seeks. If whatever you're selling will enable the sadist to wreak more havoc than usual, your match is probably made. If what you're selling expands the disparity of power between sadists and those reporting to them, or otherwise makes people more vulnerable to the sadists' punishment, you're in. Your coupe de grâce will come the moment you match your product with sadists' abilities to increase the number of people over which they have the power to inflict pain.

A Masochistic Match-Up

Playing the match game with masochists follows the same principles—sort of. It really won't matter whether your product matches the needs of other people or the organization that employs the masochist. Your product must not threaten the masochist's ability to feel miserable. It's hard for most salespeople to shift gears from how great their product will make their customers feel to pitching the fact that their products really don't make you feel any better at all.

Luckily, masochists like to feel miserable. The key word in the last sentence is "feel." Except in the most extreme cases, masochists really don't want to experience real pain and suffering. Some do, but they will not be a large part of your prospecting population. Consider how it makes the masochist feel to see others feeling good and enjoying life. As we mentioned in Chapter Three, that's your match; others feeling good so the masochist can feel self-pity. Therefore, in a curious twist of logic, you hammer home the idea of how good others will feel after the masochist buys your product. That's sure to make him or her feel miserable, and that's sure to make him or her buy.

A Paranoid Match-Up

It once again runs contrary to the paranoid person's essential nature to believe anything you say. Not because he or she is skeptical about the veracity of your product claims. Even though sales idiots and advertising morons over the years have given the human race and most of the lower forms ample cause to doubt anything a salesperson or an advertisement claims, that's not where the paranoid person gets hung up. Paranoid people don't necessarily care if what you claim about your product, company, or self is a bunch of hooey. That's not important to them. What is important to paranoid people is what you mean by what you say. In other words, paranoid people are focused like lasers on your hidden agenda. Even if you don't have one, it will be impossible to convince them.

Their suspicion is rooted not in disbelief of what others claim to be true as much as a profound and abiding belief that whatever people say is a coverup. When paranoid people talk to you on the telephone or in person they believe that you're hiding something. They believe that you have a secret and your secret has something to do with the grand conspiracy against them. Do you think you can match to that, Einstein? Or should we say, Freud?

If you are to successfully match your product to the perceptions of paranoid people your product must appear to strengthen their position to ward off the evil forces that are amassing against them. In the minds of paranoid people there are storm clouds gathering everywhere with their names on them. Your product must resemble an umbrella, a slicker, hip waders, an ecosuit, a fallout shelter, whatever. If you've properly identified paranoids among your *i*-customers you'll rapidly get a sense of how colossal they believe the impending disaster will be for them.

A Greek God or Goddess Match-Up

What do you present to someone who has everything? How do you match your products to what a person needs when the person needs nothing? It's all part of that ultimate opinion of oneself that Greek gods and goddesses share. In truth it's all an act. Those who pretend to be gods and goddesses aren't really and, at some level, they're aware of same. Nevertheless, you need to play the game around them if for no other reason than it's important to them.

Our advice is to play the mortal card. The product you offer bears tremendous benefits to the mere mortals scurrying over the face of the earth. The more you can convince a small-*g* god that your product will relieve the burden of providing for all of us mortals, the more their job becomes a skate. It's tough being god—even with a small *g*—perhaps especially with a small *g*. They sit on a throne of judgment, like Donald Trump, making life-and-death decisions about who keeps their jobs and who gets fired.

But that's the fun part. There's also answering prayers, providing for the little people, and all the minutiae that makes being a god a tough job. Match what you have to sell with easing their pain. They'll give you all of the clues you'll need. Help them to get the minutiae off their plates and the throne of judgment a nicer place to hang out and you'll have some happy *i*-god customers.

A Best Buddy Match-Up

Just as the Machiavellian is looking for power, your new best buddy is looking for a new best buddy. You wondered why he or she was so eager to schedule an appointment with you. Nobody else ever seems to be. Now you know. Friends that become closer to you than a surgical implant are not honoring even the most basic social boundaries. As we pointed out before, they might be reluctant to buy because buying means you'll go away.

With your best buddy customers the match game can become just that: a game. You can have fun with it. Make sure that they understand that once they buy from you they get to buy again. That will be tons of fun for you both. As difficult as it might be to digest, you want a long-term, lucrative relationship with all of your customers. With your *b*-customer longevity won't be a problem.

Make sure, though, that you take the multiple opportunities your buddy customer will give you to match up as many products and applications as possible. When you've sold your *b*-customer all that can be sold move on to the lead game. Have him or her match you with others in his or her organization or life who also need what you have to sell (and might also want to be his or her new buddy).

A Decent Soul Match-Up

With decent, straightforward customers you can more easily match what they really need with what your products really do. It's honest business between honest people. Not that you're ever dishonest. But dealing with a decent soul requires less monkey business and/or jumping through hoops. When you put it in perspective, your match game with a decent soul might be significantly less dramatic than it will be with a Machiavellian or a Greek god, but that can also be more refreshing.

Playing the match game between your current or prospective decent customer's needs and your product's capabilities is a way to calibrate both your product and your selling skills. It can get so wacky dealing with some of the more outrageous personality types that you forget what it's like to shoot straight. Enjoy the calm and emotionally mature interaction. Take it all in. If you're a drama-addict your foot will start to twitch and your palms will start to sweat. If you find that you can't get through the day without confronting at least one totally outrageous personality, by now you'll know where to find one and it won't be in the decent soul's office or home.

CHAPTER FOUR SUMMARY

Great products, great salespeople, and great companies won't do you a bit of good until and unless they match up with what your current or prospective customers want and need. Furthermore, the alignment needs to match your *i*-customer's sense of reality, not yours. You don't need to adjust your reality to match that of your current or prospective customers. You do need to understand their reality and translate the value and benefits of your product and working with your company into a language they will understand and appreciate.

- Shift your presentation: Many sales professionals fail to recognize that the idiots across the desk from them think $2 + 2 = 5$. Don't attempt to reeducate. The prospect's perceptions must match your proposed solution. If not, there will be no comfort achieved, and no sale closed. Translate it into his or her language and shift your presentation. It will be much easier than shifting your *i*-customer's perception.
- Match your *i*-customer's problem with your solution: Don't get hung up in semantics and situational reality. Give it to your *i*-customer the way he or she wants to hear it. Only an idiot salesperson will try to force a square peg through a round hole. The more empathic you can be the faster you'll present something acceptable to your current or prospective customers.

- Be pitch-ready: Get it done in 2 minutes and then focus on where the holes are. Your customers, idiots or otherwise, want assurance that you're not wasting their time, assurance that you're not going to damage them with your product or sales tactics, and that you'll be there when they need you. Explain why you're there, what you have to offer, who you and your company are, and what you expect to happen.
- Float trial closes: You could have your sales closed and be on your way out of your customer's office or home in a matter of minutes if you offer them the chance to buy early and often. Their hesitations become your road map to the next trial close. Learn fast as you attempt to mix and match what you're selling with what your customers will buy. Each time they pass on a trial close, pay lots of attention. Do they want more assurance about benefits, values, or emotional rewards for buying?
- Be ready for the weird: As always, you'll deal with a zoo full of wild characters. Be ready for them. When need be, become a wild character yourself. As long as you keep playing the match game, you're headed in the right direction. Just make sure your attempted matches resonate with the diverse personalities you're faced with. Don't suggest a match that will make Machiavellians feel badly about themselves.
- Be kid-smart: We can learn much from them. Their matches are sometimes incredible stretches. But they sometimes work. Close, close, and close again—until the deal is closed. Children are relentless. Kids are surely not the ones who taught us to give up as we got older. We need to pay less attention to whoever threw the wet blanket on our optimism and pay more attention to kids.

Your tool kit is expanding. Your skills are sharpening. You're finding more and more common ground jointly occupied by your inner idiot and your customer's inner idiot. You're also finding more and more reasonable ways to connect with your customers as you match problems with solutions. As brilliant as you're becoming at all this you still need to develop a keen sense for when it's Showtime. The last thing you want is for the curtain to go up before you're ready.

5

STEP FIVE: SHOWTIME

Idiots love a floor show. No matter how fabulous your merchandise and services are you're not going to sell as much or as often if you're bo-o-o-oring. Step five is your union card for the entertainment business. Many people consider selling to be 10 percent information and 90 percent presentation. They have a point, even if their numbers are skewed. We doubt any major university study has ever been conducted to find out how much of the selling process is entertainment versus education. But we'll lay odds that edutainment beats straight dissemination of data any day.

The value of entertaining your audience is nothing new. However, as the proliferating number of channels available on cable and satellite television indicates, there is a wide range of subjects that a wide range of people find entertaining. Some watch reruns of Gilligan's Island, some watch prime-time dramas on the major networks or HBO, some watch Animal Planet or the Cooking Channel, while others watch the Golf Channel. We won't be surprised to see a Law and Order Channel or a CSI Channel in the not-too-distant future. Whatever it is, it's all entertainment.

Please note that we've temporarily altered our vocabulary. In keeping with our Showtime theme, we've changed the term "customer" to "audience." When thinking of the entertainment value of your presentations it's helpful to think of your customers as your audience. Recent research indicates that as many as 80 percent of all audiences surveyed make their purchasing decisions based on how impressed they are by the presentation.

Sales leadership expert, keynote speaker, and author, Danny Cox (www.dannycox.com) is often heard to tell the tale of two aging character actors who came to work for him as real estate salespeople in southern California's San Fernando Valley back in the 1960s. They couldn't seem to get the hang of selling. In a stroke of brilliance Danny handed them their sales manuals. "Gentlemen, here is your script," Danny told them. "Study it hard because the customers already know their lines." A glow of familiarity came over their faces. After that they no longer went on sales calls. They went on auditions. Suddenly the old character actors became selling superstars—even if they never reached that status on stage or screen.[1]

The issue of being impressed by your presentation begs the obvious question, "What do you mean by impressed?" It could and probably does mean just about anything. Is the audience impressed with the salesperson's wardrobe? Grooming? Funny accent? University degrees? Eloquent manner of speaking? Height? Weight? What? One thing's for sure: Great content never saves a poor presentation. An audience isn't totally impressed by facts and figures unless you're selling to a CPA, in which case a little pizzazz never hurts, anyway. (Make sure your jokes are math jokes.) All your preparation, connecting, skilled questioning, listening, mixing, and matching won't amount to much unless you get your current or prospective audience's attention, keep it, and make it a memorable experience.

This doesn't mean you offer your audience bogus merchandise or service. Being a great entertainer might impress some audiences enough to buy once, twice, or maybe even three times. They might even buy a time or two after they've figured out you're selling junk. But you're only as good as your last show, and folks get tired of the same old same old. Even *i*-audiences can be a tough crowd to play to after a while. All the entertainment in the world won't make up for disappointing results over time. It's more likely that your audiences

[1]Cox, D., & Hoover, J. (2002). *Leadership When the Heat's On* (2nd ed.). New York: McGraw-Hill.

will keep buying if your product is terrific—even after your act is a little worn out.

ENTERTAINMENT VERSUS BOREDOM

Sales trainers often teach that people want three things: to be listened to, to be appreciated, and to be entertained. Maybe yes. Maybe no. But whether listening in and of itself will make a sale is immaterial. The fact that listening is a core skill in the detective and anthropological study of your current and prospective audiences notwithstanding, it can't hurt. People will be particularly impressed by your active listening when and if they don't feel listened to by others. If they are more or less transparent to the rest of the world until you walk in the door, you're a welcome sight. That's not a bad thing for sales professionals.

The more you make it all about them, the better. This seems contradictory to some. You're supposed to be a great entertainer. Doesn't that mean being on stage, in the spotlight, the microphone in your hand, and all eyes on you? Sure it does—if you're Wayne Newton. Your audience didn't pay a cover charge with a two-drink minimum to hear what you have to say. Having said that, the reason people go to shows is to be entertained. Being entertained usually means getting their minds off of their troubles. One of the fastest and most effective ways to do that is to make them part of the show—or make them the whole show, whichever works best.

Appreciation is similar to entertainment in that the appreciation you bestow upon your audience is beneficial to you in direct proportion to how underappreciated they feel in other areas of their lives. Your audience members might have had a blow-up with their spouses or kids that morning, or both. Perhaps they had a flat tire on the way to work. Maybe their team lost the big game last night. Work demands are up and/or compensation is down. Who knows what has dampened your audience's day before you arrived. Making your audience feel appreciated will never hurt you. If they're having a great day already you don't want to be a wet blanket. Even if they're sky-high emotionally, showing appreciation through good listening skills will be icing on the cake. So, be entertainingly appreciative.

The sales trainers who talk about customers' needs to be listened to, to be appreciated, and to be entertained are trying to tap into Abraham Maslow's hierarchy of needs. Perhaps not tap into so much as to scratch the surface or rub up against. Your audiences, be they idiots, Machiavellians, sadists, masochists, paranoids, Greek gods, emotionally needy, or ordinarily decent folks, all subscribe to Abraham Maslow's hierarchy of needs—either consciously or unconsciously, deliberately or against their will. Physiological needs are at the base of the pyramid; then come the safety needs, then love needs, esteem, and finally, self-actualization needs sit at the top. To stay alive you need to deal with the bottom issues first. Self-actualization will be great as long as you're not starving to death or being otherwise killed in the meantime.

ENTERTAINMENT VERSUS FILLING NEEDS

What are you supposed to do with this information? Do you feed your audiences, clothe them, and give them shelter to satisfy their physiological needs? Do you fight their battles for them or beat up the office or neighborhood bully to fulfill their safety needs? Do you tell them how attractive, intelligent, and talented they are to fulfill their esteem needs? Do you introduce them to your personal mountaintop guru to help them fulfill their self-actualization needs?

Physiological Needs

Taking your audience to lunch is a way of fulfilling a physiological need. It's not as though your audiences can't buy their own lunches, but lunch on somebody else's dime is always a treat. Taking an audience out to lunch or dinner, or even bringing a box of donuts or chocolates with you on your sales call, is not a bad idea, unless your audience is on a torture diet. We hope you have enough research data to avoid that faux pas before you make it. In our culture, in most cases, being fed means being nurtured and cared for. However, no amount of food will substitute for your need to be entertaining. If anything beats dinner all by itself, it's dinner and a show.

Clothing is another physiological need you can address for your current and prospective audiences. Many companies embroider their name and logo on golf shirts, hats, sweaters, and jackets. Umbrellas are big in damp climates. Delivering the wardrobe swag or food and beverage to your audience's doorstep serves as a token of your appreciation and makes them feel thought about. Remember to make the food, beverage, and swag as entertaining as possible in content, delivery, or both.

Safety Needs

Safety is not an area that a sales professional customarily delves into. Or is it? The answer depends on your definition of safety. On first blush, the Maslowian category of safety implies physical safety. Unless you're selling safety products you might be risking a potential back injury by stretching to connect physical safety with what you're selling. If you have the good fortune to be on a Caribbean cruise with a current or prospective customer when he or she falls overboard, our advice is to rescue that person personally. He or she will have a tough time not buying from you after that. Alas, such opportunities to exploit the safety need are few and far between. Fortunately, you can tweak the definition of safety a little and make it come out in your favor more often.

For example, make safety synonymous with job security. If you're selling consumer products, make safety synonymous with preserving your audiences' relationships with spouses or other significant people in their lives. In other words, you can make safety (as it relates to your product) synonymous with emotional safety. Presenting a compelling (and entertaining) argument that what you're selling will help your current or prospective audiences solidify or even enhance their professional or social positions in their companies or communities will be tough for your competition to beat. In other words, selling a sense of security invokes the safety need.

Love Needs

Showing appreciation to someone who doesn't otherwise feel appreciated fills a sense of deficiency in Maslowian love needs. Listening to someone who doesn't feel otherwise listened to tends to fill the same need. Trying to convince your current or prospective audiences that you love them might be a bit extreme. But following through on what you promise and treating them with respect and dignity, together with listening, being attentive and appreciative will demonstrate better behavior than most loving couples can lay claim to.

Be careful that you don't stumble upon a love-starved client. You might have trouble extracting yourself from a nonprofessional and possibly unholy alliance. We've seen it happen. An attentive and appreciative sales professional, even with completely honest intentions, becomes the love slave of an audience who feels the salesperson is more attentive, appreciative, respectful, and a better listener than the audience's significant idiot. While all that might be true, we strongly advise you not to go there. You don't need a deadly attraction in your life. No commission is worth that. Besides, you'll probably wind up giving it all back in the divorce anyway.

Esteem Needs

The key here is to remember it's not your ego that needs stroking. If you would spend your last dollar on something to make you thinner, taller, younger, and better looking all around, so would most other people. There's nothing wrong with appealing to your audience's ego. In fact, that will set the stage nicely. Cast a little spotlight in his or her direction, add a little applause, and suddenly your audience is the entertainment. Do you ever notice how audience members who are brought onstage during Las Vegas shows never seem to fully appreciate how foolish they look? That's because it doesn't matter, as long as they're in the show.

If looking ridiculous was a deterrent for the average person there'd be no reality television, no matter how cheap it is to produce. You can put your existing audiences in the show by featuring them in newsletters or other materials you publish, on billboards, or in other advertising. Of course, you need their permission for these things. But with a country full of people willing to swap spouses, expose their half-naked bodies on desert islands, and engage in any number of undignified activities in front of millions of voyeuristic television viewers, chances are good that your audience will be up for a picture and a gushing caption in your newsletter.

True, a sales presentation is your showtime, but you'll have more to show for it at the end of the day if you can convince your current and prospective audiences that it's their showtime. If you can't repress your need to be in the limelight, find a karaoke bar after work. After building your audience's self-esteem all day why not go out afterward and place yours in serious jeopardy? If you're ever in a karaoke bar with any of your audiences make sure you tell them how brilliantly they sing. Invoke the golf clause: Lose. Never outshine your audiences, no matter how dim they are.

Self-Actualization Needs

We can't say whether your audience is interested in self-actualization. We're not all that sure about you, either. Many of us carbon-based life forms are scurrying around on this planet just trying to make ends meet and keep the wolf away from the door. Self-actualization is pretty heady stuff. It's sort of like an elective course in life after all the core requirements have been completed. That was Maslow's whole point to begin with.

Physiological needs are required courses. We eat or die. The same applies to safety. We stay safe or we get hurt. Now things become more discretionary. We find love or we're lonely. We build self-esteem or we spend a lot of time alone with someone we don't like very much. Finally, whether or not we become everything our Creator divined that we could become, who's gonna know? But, if self-actualization is important to your audiences be prepared to listen and nod to their tales of spiritual growth and universal enlightenment. In fact, you might want to try some of that yourself. There isn't a salesperson alive who wouldn't benefit from a direct line to God.

BE ENERGIZED

Some say that as much as 80 percent of all lost sales are directly related to a poor and/or underenergized presentation. Whether you elect to deal with the complete complexity of Maslow's hierarchy of needs or use the Cliffs Notes version (listen, appreciate, and entertain), all great presentations must be energized. Quiet or loud, each moment should be energized. But energy can be ephemeral, meaning it will come and go quickly if you don't plan strategically to make sure it lasts as long as you need it to. It's all in your timing, content, and delivery.

You don't necessarily want to leave the presentation with gas in your tank, either. Commercial pilots and their flight engineers attempt to calculate the precise amount of fuel for a flight because they need to dump any excess prior to landing. In a perfect world, the pilots and flight planners would load the precise amount of fuel, and land with dry tanks.

As a contingency, however, they add 30 to 60 minutes worth of additional fuel before takeoff in case the planned landing site needs to be changed or the plane for some reason needs to stay in a prolonged holding pattern. That's why they are forced to dump excess fuel before landing. Since you're not flying a jet full of passengers we suggest that you leave your prospect's office or sales presentation with nothing but fumes in your tank. Burn what you have in front of your audience and refuel later. As athletes and coaches say, don't leave anything on the field or court.

Pace Yourself

Don't begin at full throttle or you won't have anywhere to go. Build highs and lows throughout your presentation for emphasis. Use silence to emphasize your key selling points and add dramatic effect. Silence also gives your audience a chance to tell you how much they love your product or to voice their objections. Either way, you won't know which card to play next until your audience fills the silence. Active listening means being engaged physically as you listen. Lean forward, make eye contact, and drink in what's being said. That's energized silence.

Telephone Energy

If you must make your presentation over the telephone it should be brief and well energized. Start the presentation with something that will get the telephone audience's attention, such as a powerful statement of intent for your presentation. Use your 2-minute drill. State your objective. Remember to be bold and direct. Arouse your audience's curiosity. Next, provide exactly the same rapid-fire information you provide in your face-to-face presentation. This isn't a game of horseshoes. You can't just get close. You need to knock it out of the park. Finally, recap and retell your audience what you've already told them. When dealing over the telephone make sure your presentation is clear, concise, and covers all the points you've strategically planned to cover—unless, of course, your customer bites on your first close. In that case, shut up.

RAZZLE-DAZZLE THEM

Now that you've decided to knock your audiences' socks off, dazzle them. How do your audiences remember you and your product once you leave their offices or homes? What memory marks do you leave behind? Your presentation should be heavy on the memorable and light on the predictable. We highly recommend being less predictable. Most salespeople's presentations all look the same, whether they're working or not. It may be time to freshen yours up.

You may be in a rut. If you are, your presentation will come off looking and sounding stale. Maybe that's because it is. You will know it is getting stale and boring when your audience starts yawning or when they leave their seats and never return. It's especially humiliating when your audience leaves you babbling in his or her office and goes home.

When we say razzle-dazzle, we're simply referring to anything that will make your presentation stand out. A great presentation can overcome an audience's concerns regarding price, quality, and even the salesperson's credibility. Although we never recommend using a dazzling presentation to pawn off bad merchandise or inferior services, if you've ever purchased bad merchandise or inferior services based on a dazzling presentation, you know how persuasive razzle-dazzle can be. We recommend that you put razzle-dazzle to good use selling your superior product.

The swag and food we referred to earlier are forms of razzle-dazzle. If you have any Super Bowl tickets to spare, that wouldn't hurt either. Razzle-dazzle doesn't sell, though. You do. But a little razzle-dazzle will get people to look at you when they might not have before. Some salespeople put a fifty-dollar bill in a letter to prospective audiences to invoke guilt. "How can the idiot pocket a fifty and not agree to hear my pitch?" they reason. Whatever it takes. Once you have someone's attention, pitch quickly, effectively, and close early and often.

Be More Than Bold and Outrageous

Many believe that success is reserved for the bold and outrageous. If that were so, why do so many bold and outrageous people drive old cars and have skinny children? Never forget that beneath all that boldness and outrageousness there needs to be solid selling skills. Also, never forget that those great selling skills won't amount to anything if you have no one to sell to. Your reason for being bold and outrageous is to get your audience's attention. The two work together. But you first need an audience.

For some, just getting on the phone and calling prospects is bold and outrageous. If you're an introvert, and many sales professionals are, it's all you can do to pick up the receiver and punch numbers into the telephone. That's bold. To actually make those calls in the numbers necessary to meet your sales goals can be downright outrageous. If the effort and stamina required to make those calls is so intense, why would you squander the opportunity when someone agrees to see you?

Boldness and outrageousness are in the eye of the beholder. You want to get your audiences' attention. But you don't want to discredit yourself in the process. As you learn more about the people you're working with, mostly through your keen detective and anthropological work, use that information to determine where their boundaries of normality are. Then you can push the boundaries in whatever way you think will amuse and entertain them. With some folks a big push is okay. With others all you might be able to get away with is a little nudge now and then. Either way, you don't want to leave them where you found them.

Engage Them

Once your incredible talents as a bold and outrageous entertainer get someone's attention, engage them quickly. Engagement, the way we're using the term, means presentation with participation. Keep your audience involved. You must avoid giving your audience an opportunity to disconnect. Use all media available to you to stimulate and maintain interest and make your presentation consistent with the style or personality of your audience. Just because your material and presentation are entertaining to you doesn't mean they will automatically resonate with your audience.

PRESENTING IN STYLE

You may have to alter your style of presentation to match your audience's style of receiving information. If your audience is visually oriented be sure and include more pictures, charts, and graphs in your presentations. Listen to the way your audience describes things. Do they say, "The way we see it," or "We can't see how that will . . . ," or "From where we're sitting that looks like . . ." Those are all cues that he or she is visually oriented. It's time for the visual stimulation of eye candy.

If your audience is made up of thinking (cognitive), pragmatic types, they will say things like, "We don't think . . . ," "The way we figure it, . . . ," or "That doesn't make sense to us." Be sure to allow a cognitive audience time to think things through and ask questions between points of your presentation. Their wheels are turning fast as you are presenting. Don't overwhelm a cognitive audience with too much show and tell. Throw out your pitch and let them ponder. It's time for the intellectual stimulation of brain candy. If your audience makes comments like, "It sounds to us like . . ." or "The way we hear it . . ." it's time for the auditory stimulation of ear candy.

With an impatient, A-type personality, get your presentation moving quickly to how your product can provide immediate solutions to current situations—don't lollygag. The A-type personality is looking for speed. Even though A-type personalities want you to get to the point quickly, you can still knock their socks off with how you present your material. Even concrete and purely logical audiences, the type who want you to prove it to them deductively, like your deductive reasoning to be entertaining. It's a way of honoring your audience to first identify their style and then adjust your presentation accordingly.

PRESENTING WITH STRUCTURE

Your presentation can't be a haphazard jumble of eye, brain, and ear candy. It must have a beginning, middle, and an end. It must have a point like a sharpened pencil, provide solutions, benefits, and scratch where it itches. A great presentation isn't just a commercial about your product, yourself, or your company. It is a compelling story of what separates you from your competition, and how your product will make a difference. How will your audience's lives be transformed after they buy from you?

Every presentation must have a purpose and direction or it will quickly turn into social conversation. How would Bruce Springsteen go over if he came out on stage, sat down, and had a 90-minute chat with the audience? You'd be surprised how many sales professionals purposefully engage in social chatter, hoping that somewhere in the middle of the conversation a sale might somehow happen. It's amazing how many great conversational-style salespeople have skinny kids and drive old cars.

PRESENTING WITH TECHNOLOGY

Technology can be a great tool in your presentation. But be sure you don't focus so much on the technical stimulation that you lose connection with your audience. Be certain you balance high tech with high touch. Many sales professionals who use laptop computers or PowerPoint presentations have a tendency to go as long as 15 to 20 minutes without ever looking at their audience. As we've stressed all along, you need visual, auditory, and kinesthetic feedback from your audiences. Feedback will provide you with critical clues that will let you know if you are on the right track or if your presentation is spinning somewhere out in space.

You've done too much good work in the previous steps preparing your pitch, discovering your audience's needs, and building relationships to blow it now with a boring, low-energy, and/or irrelevant presentation. Your presentation should stimulate interest and constructive conversation—conversation that leads to the grand prize—an order, a signature, or a signature on an order. Earth to salesperson: That won't happen if you unplug and/or lose connection with your audience.

REHEARSALS

Consider those proverbial out-of-towners in New York City who walked around for hours trying to find Carnegie Hall. Finally the wife spotted a man carrying a violin case. "Excuse me, sir," she called out. "Can you tell us how to get to Carnegie Hall?" Without batting an eye, the man with the violin case replied, "Practice, practice, practice."

That preparation stuff from Chapter One just won't go away. A well-prepared presentation lets your audiences know that you value their time. Prepare, polish, pitch, and repeat as often as possible. Pace yourself and rehearse the crescendos that increase the impact of your pitch. Practice using stillness and listening opportunities as spacers to add effect. You'll be more entertaining than you know. Rehearse, rehearse, and rehearse some more.

Rehearse in front of a friendly-yet-honest audience. Record your presentation. Listen to yourself. Are you compelling, interesting? Are you believable? Videotape yourself. It may be an eye opener. It may be the best training video you ever watch. Ask yourself, "Would I purchase from me?" Remember what you are watching is what your audience is seeing. Your audience is sizing you up. How you present yourself is critical. The way you look and sound are more important than the words you use in determining whether your audience buys. The ratio is 93 percent to seven percent, remember? If you mean business, look and sound like you mean business. Everything counts, and your audience will notice everything.

MORE LESSONS FROM CHILDREN

With kids it's always showtime. The legend of kids putting on a show in a barn is more than the stuff of 1930s Hollywood. Given the opportunity, kids will dramatize anything. They haven't had their imaginations snuffed out yet. Their mantra: If we put on a show the audience will come. It's the *Field of Dreams* factor. As a result, kids make incredible presentations. That may be the first clue as to why they get what they want so much of the time. Their presentations are naturally created using curiosity, imagination, and high energy.

Kids are unapologetically bold and outrageous and know how to get our attention because they study us so intensely. They do whatever it takes to generate a focused audience, and only then do they begin to present their case for what they want. They make it fun and entertaining. Kids rehearse their presentations, in real time, maybe 100 times a day. They rehearse on their dolls and stuffed toys. They rehearse on the dog. (Cats know better and hide.) They put their dolls, stuffed toys, and dogs into the show. When it comes to entertaining, kids are the complete package. They have purpose, direction, and a clear agenda. They know how to get you engaged.

Kids are focused like laser beams on what they want. Their focus doesn't drift to the right or the left until they've burned a hole right through your skull. Kids aren't concerned about making mistakes—they just keep presenting. Kids' presentations are memorable and to the point. Yes, indeed. If we could sell with half the sincerity, conviction, and relentlessness of a child, we'd all be gazillionaires.

PERSONALITY-BASED ENTERTAINMENT

Have you noticed a pattern in each chapter? We never want to neglect the more eccentric and unusual folks you must deal with in the world of professional sales. We mentioned the Type-A personality earlier in this chapter; there is no end to the variations on the humanity theme. The same principle applies to our old friends the Machiavellians, sadists, masochists, paranoids, Greek gods, buddies, and decently good folks.

Showtime for the Machiavellian

This show had better feature the Machiavellian in the starring role. No best supporting actor or actress for the Machiavellian. There is one star, one name at the top of the credits, that's it. Remember the primetime sitcom, Laverne and Shirley? Billing battles were nothing new to Hollywood in the 1970s. But when Penny Marshall's people went to war with Cindy Williams' people over billing, their compromise was unique. Penny Marshall's name appeared on the screen first, reading left to right, but Cindy Williams' name, although on the right, appeared higher on the screen.

It would be interesting to see how the titles appeared in countries that read right to left. Be that as it may, when dealing with a Machiavellian audience make sure the Machiavellian's name is both first and above anyone else's. That's your sure-fire road to success with a Machiavellian. The plotline must feature the Machiavellian overcoming all odds and obstacles to reach the pinnacle of success. That's the show of shows for a Machiavellian.

Showtime for the Sadist

A snuff film might be a breach of your ethical construct. But get as close to it as you can and still be able to live with yourself. The sadist is entertained by the pain and suffering of others, especially if he or she is the perpetrator of said pain and suffering. You must obviously cast the sadist in the power position vis-à-vis the rest of the cast. The disparity of power is very important.

Being the storyteller, you can keep yourself out of the sadist's line of fire to some degree; perhaps long enough to get his or her order and make good your escape while he or she is hammering someone else. We joke about the number of S&M magazines and videos on the market. But there might be a bigger market for sadists and masochists in business than we realize. Although they may hide it well, we wonder how many of our audiences are made up of sadists in business casual. It's just one more thing to make us say, "Hm-m-m-m."

Showtime for the Masochist

Have you ever been at wit's end, frustrated to the point that you actually chased your audience away? It's not a recommended practice unless you *want* to have skinny kids and drive an old car. But we've heard reports from some sales professionals that, after chasing customers away, some of the customers came back practically begging to buy. It sounds like a dream or a fantasy floating on gossamer wings, but it actually happens.

Using this method to ferret out the masochists in your audiences will probably produce a desirable and an undesirable result. You may indeed identify and sell to your masochists. But you'll probably lose everybody else as a customer in the process. That's not a risk we recommend you take. However, if your audience is aggravating the snot out of you for no apparent reason and acting as if they want to be slapped silly, you may have a masochist on your hands. You might try mentioning a couple of reasons not to buy. If he or she gets increasingly aroused go to your close before things get physical.

Showtime for the Paranoid

Oliver Stone has made a career out of conspiracy theories. So can you. If your research and inquiry has confirmed that you have a bona fide paranoid personality on your hands, start writing a part for a victim. The victim is not you. It's your audience. You're not the victimizer either. Everyone else on the planet is. If you've seen many Oliver Stone films you know that victimizers in conspiracy stories don't really need to demonstrate any palpable motivation. They're simply evildoers. What makes them evil? The fact that they want to victimize the paranoid, of course. Beyond that, who needs a reason?

It's sort of like the hapless boss. Not any particular boss. Conventional wisdom tends to cast all bosses as idiots.[2] More than shameless self-promotion, the whole concept of the idiot boss serves to illustrate that character development arcs don't apply to bosses.

Whereas any other character is required to change somehow between the beginning and the end of the story, a boss is assumed to be a boob from page one or frame one and will most likely still be a boob if he or she survives through the end of the story. Likewise, the paranoids in your audiences will be victims from page one through the end of the story, and their oppressors will remain oppressors throughout. You could say that paranoids have vivid imaginations, imagining conspiracies where none exist. In truth, given their shallow or nonexistent character development, you could question the depth and dimension of their imaginations. They do imagine the conspiracies in vivid detail, though. Give paranoid personalities points for originality and creativity.

Showtime for the Greek God or Goddess

Picture palaces in the clouds, enormous stone pillars with eloquent capitals, and elaborate thrones with majestic, robed characters serenely observing the mere mortals far below. Greek gods and goddesses prefer their films to be directed by Cecil B. DeMille. So, pull your riding boots over your puffy pants and grab your leather crop. It's time to produce an epic.

Epics are epics because they have epic proportions. That means big. If you're playing to an audience of Greek gods and/or goddesses you need to portray them as bigger than life. Their powers are prac-

---

[2]Hoover, J. (2003). *How to Work for an Idiot: Survive and Thrive without Killing Your Boss.* Franklin Lakes, NJ: Career Press.

tically beyond description. The only reason their characteristics remain within the realm of description is so you can describe them, much to the delight of this small-*h* heavenly audience. The product you're selling needs to be woven in as a prop. Not just any prop. It needs to be as significant as Neptune's trident or Zeus' thunderbolts. Neptune can always be interested in a shiny new trident and Zeus keeps using up his thunderbolts. There you are with what they want and need to stay in character. Need we say more?

Showtime for Your Best Buddy

This could be your fifteenth season of *Friends*. You might feel you're in rerun hell keeping this act up. No matter what your emotionally needy audience goes through, your story always ends with you and your buddy riding off into the sunset side by side. Or so you spin the yarn. Somewhere in the mix you'll be providing products that actually enhance and embellish your buddy's personal and/or professional life. But don't let that get in the way of a good story about pals forever.

Regardless of the actual content of your performance and the business you need to get done in order to feed your kids and put gas in that old car, would it hurt for you to rhetorically wrap your arm around your best buddy's shoulder, walk across that rain-soaked tarmac, and say, "Louie, I think this is the beginning of a beautiful friendship?" You'll be in black and white, but your audience won't even notice.

Showtime for the Decent Soul

As appealing as show business seems to the average bear it will come as an enormous relief to just be real with a customer for a change—even an *i*-customer. There are more decent souls out there than you might realize. If there weren't, Jimmy Stewart and Bob Hope would have never become so obscenely wealthy. Of course there's a new generation coming up that probably wouldn't have bought into *Mr. Smith Goes to Washington* or *Little Miss Marker*.

Be that as it may, there are still lots of folks, young and old, who want the straight poop. Just because it's clean and wholesome doesn't mean it can't be entertaining. Consider Will Smith. Although we don't have the statistical evidence to prove it, we'll venture that you're better off being direct, sincere, and honest than being a bad actor. At least if you start out being genuine and authentic you won't get thrown out. Your audience might go to sleep, but you won't have offended anyone. When your audience wakes up you still have a chance. The next move is up to you.

CHAPTER FIVE SUMMARY

Selling is Showtime. Think of yourself as a clown at a kid's birthday party. Be as outrageous as the kid. Use uncommon sense to open common minds and poke around in there. It might be the kid's party, but you're selling the cake. Good frosting never made a cake less desirable unless it was the wrong frosting. Your choice of entertainment style and content must resonate with your audience or they'll change channels.

- Selling involves entertainment or, at the very least, avoiding boredom: As such, you need to think of your current or prospective customers as your audience. You're not going on a sales call, you're going on an audition, and you want to be cast in the role of the successful sales professional.
- Entertainment plus education equals edutainment: That's the business you're in. Making the sale, especially to a clueless audience, is a matter of teaching them the information they need to buy from you. You must do that in a way that keeps your audience's interest or the information will be wasted.
- Rehearsal is your secret weapon: It's no secret really, but as little as most salespeople prepare, you'd think it was a great secret. Rehearsal makes you intimately familiar with your script. Being intimately familiar with your lines makes you confident. In the words of actor Jack Palance on an old Mennen Skin Bracer commercial, "Confidence is sexy."
- Every audience has a personality: Abraham Maslow identified the human hierarchy of needs. At the bottom are physiological needs. Next are safety needs. Next are love needs. Above love needs are esteem needs. On top are self-actualization needs. You need to determine where on your audience's hierarchy of

needs you can enter their world and write your script accordingly.

- Play to the personality: As usual, you need to be sensitive to your audience's personality and tell the story with which they will resonate and within which they can cast themselves. Tell the wrong story to the wrong audience or cast them in a role that contradicts the image they have of themselves and you can forget the sale. Be entertaining, but be accurate.

Coming up next: It's gut-check time at the OK Corral as you saddle up and ask for the business. Will your *i*-customer give you the business or give you the business? It depends on how well you've been paying attention. Stay tuned.

6

STEP SIX: ASK FOR THE BUSINESS

Every professional salesperson in history has been trained to ask for the order. Only an idiot salesperson will just keep talking until the customer interrupts and begs to buy. Then again, you'd be surprised how many idiots are selling for a living. This is a case where you don't want your inner idiot to resonate too much with your customers' inner idiots. Worse yet, you don't want to slip into idiocy at precisely the same moment that our current or prospective customer has an idiot moment. If you're too bashful to ask for the order because that opens up the possibility for the customer to say "No," do you really expect your *i*-customer to come to your rescue by saying, "Please buy from me?"

If you think we're kidding, how many times have you kept talking even after your current or prospective customer has tried to interrupt you to buy? You've probably seen it happen with others, but never considered that it might be happening to you. We should more correctly say that you might have never considered that you might be doing it. It happens all the time:

"Okay," says the customer. "I'm ready to buy."

"No problem," you reply. "Just wait until I've finished this pitch."

"Seriously," the customer interrupts again. "I'm ready to buy now. Just show me where to sign."

"Keep your shirt on," you snap, showing your agitation with these constant interruptions. "You said you'd give me 30 minutes and we have 15 minutes left. Now sit there and be quiet until I'm finished."

Years ago one of the authors was involved with the Maytag Company in Newton, Iowa. Maytag trained its sales representatives in a unique way. When video technology was still in the early Beta format sales trainers at the Maytag training center in Newton videotaped their reps giving mock sales presentations. Then they played back the tapes to an audience full of their peers. Each rep in the audience held a little toy cricket clicker, the kind you click with your thumb. (They were made of tin in those days, and if you weren't careful it could draw blood; toy safety has come a long way since then.)

All danger notwithstanding, when the sales rep on the videotape reached a point in the presentation when the customer appeared ready to buy, his or her peers and trainers would start clicking the crickets. Almost without exception the noise from the crickets in the auditorium was deafening before the rep on the tape ever attempted a close. You can see how that might get the message across. There was the rep, caught on videotape, jabbering away long after the time was right to ask for the order.

Opportunity after opportunity came and went and the reps usually jawed right through them. Unfortunately, those were the days before handheld air horns were popular. Instead of the bucolic sound of crickets reminding the trainees of their verbal incontinence, a dozen air horns blowing in their ears might have left them a lot wiser a lot sooner. Deaf maybe, but definitely wiser.

CECO

Close early and close often. We say it so often that we might as well just use the acronym CECO. Current and prospective customers might not be ready to buy when you try your first close, but how will you know if you don't ask? Asking for something increases the chances you'll get it if only because *i*-customers have trouble reading their own minds, much less yours. To put it another way, idiot customers can listen to you tout the benefits and value of your product all day and still not have a clue that you want them to buy it unless you tell them. If you've attempted several closes, and they still don't realize you want them to buy, it's time to polish that pitch or rewrite it altogether.

Despite how much sense it makes to articulate your desires for an order, simply asking for it has always been and remains the number-one weakness of most salespeople. Yet a salesperson's income will ultimately be determined by his or her ability to get the customer to sign on the dotted line. For average and underachieving salespeople, locating and even qualifying prospects is much easier than asking the prospect for business. Our advice to professional salespeople 21 or older: Get over it. Better to ask too soon and too often than not to ask at all. Asking makes it easier for the customer to buy. It's the natural conclusion to your pitch—not the final conflict.

Our friend, Roger DiSilvestro, is the CEO of Athlon Sports Publishing. As one of the country's top experts in commissioned sales leadership, Roger notes in sales meetings and private conversations that there are three things he expects to hear from a current or prospective customer (in ascending desirability):

- "Roger, leave town. No, leave the country. Better yet, leave the state. Your pitch is the most ridiculous thing we've ever heard."
- "Roger, that's all very interesting. Thanks for a terrific pitch. We'll call you."
- "Roger, is there any limit to the amount of money we can spend with your company?"

Obviously, Roger coaches his salespeople to ascend from the first bullet to the third bullet as quickly as possible. He coaches his sales professionals to use comedic comments like this one to endear themselves to their customers. He actually told a group of grumpy clients one day that those were the three things he expected to hear from them. They broke up laughing and the entire atmosphere changed. Roger's motto—"Blow them away with something funny." It eases your nerves and loosens up their clamshell brains. The knowledge that you have something well-prepared and clever to say makes going into the presentation less terrifying.

We could have included Roger's comments about humor in Chapter Five about entertainment, but humor serves the sales professional as much as it serves the customers. If that fear-of-rejection thing is looming large over your head and causing you to avoid asking for the order, humor can put you at ease. Somehow, people seem less threatening and feel less threatened when everybody has a smile on their face. You can see how using Roger's brand of self-deprecating humor on the front end can speed things toward a positive conclusion.

Go in prepared and rehearsed. Asking for the order isn't something you'll do on the spur of the moment if you can work up the courage. You've prepared thoroughly enough to be confident with your humorous comment. The same goes for your first close, 90 seconds into your pitch. The great sales people don't wait to see what the mood is. They use their experience and skill to create the proper mood for closing the deal. If you aren't prepared with your pitch from A to Z, alpha to omega, inside and out, top to bottom, soup to nuts, you're not ready to work. Hoping the mood will be right is the same thing as handing all of the power to influence your environment over to your *i*-customer. You're at your current or prospective customer's mercy enough as it is without tipping the scales further in their favor.

ASKING IS ACTION

Asking is a verb. It implies action. It's not passive. You are asking your current or prospective customers to take action through your well-thought-out, clear, and concise requests. If you don't believe that what you're selling will produce the benefits you claim it will produce, you shouldn't be selling it. So why wouldn't you actively and enthusiastically pursue a course of action that would enhance your current or prospective customer's ultimate well-being? Before we venture too far from the wisdom of Roger DiSilvestro, his take on the moral certitude of selling is classic. He stands in front of sales meetings and sits across the desk from individual salespeople he's coaching and tells them that selling is nothing less than an act of compassion. If you don't believe that, why are you in this business?

Knowing that the action you're taking by asking for the order is going to enhance someone's personal and/or professional life, as well as your own, why would you hesitate to ask? Writing in the online publication, *E Summation* (March 2001), Auren Hoffman said "Wayne Gretzky's saying that you miss 100 percent of the shots you don't take is an adjunct to the [maxim] 'perfect is the enemy of the good.' Gretzky is saying try, take your best shot (literally and figuratively), and if it doesn't work take another shot. Don't try to be perfect all the time—try to be good and be good a lot. Because if you don't take a shot simply because it is not a high percentage shot, it could really be a missed opportunity."

Taking action doesn't guarantee that you'll cash in on the opportunity. Asking for the order doesn't mean you'll get it. But not taking action will guarantee the opportunity will be missed. Not asking for the order will guarantee that you won't get it. There are always exceptions. Hope springs eternal. That's why there's a lottery in most states. There can always be that one-in-a-million exception where the customer interrupts you, leaps over the desk, tackles you, pins you to the floor, and screams in your face, demanding to buy this instant. But do you want to base your professional success and personal happiness on something that might happen once every blue moon? Can you truly live in the exception column? Given the choice, will you choose to be an idiot? Guess what—the choice is yours every day.

ASK WITH CONFIDENCE

You must expect to win the customer. Expect to get what you ask for. Ask as if it were impossible for you to fail. Be direct and bottom line. Tell your *i*-customer, "I'm going to be direct and bottom line with you." What do you think your customer will say: "No, I would rather you just beat around the bush and be generally vague and evasive." If your current or prospective customer is a true idiot he or she might be thinking that, but would never say it aloud. At the end of the day any customer will appreciate frankness and directness.

Your customers ultimately want the bottom line, so the fact that they'll allow you to keep talking and not ask you to leave is a way of granting you permission. Now that you have their permission don't be an idiot and beat around the bush. Be clear, concise, and give them a compelling reason to not only purchase what you're selling, but to purchase it from you. Solve their problem. Make it easy for your customers to say yes.

Some Steps to Confidence

Even when you don't feel confident it's important to look confident. We're not advising you to be fraudulent about it. But coming off as apologetic won't instill confidence in your current or prospective customers. The appearance of confidence is extremely important. The way to appear more confident is to focus on the little things that you're totally confident you can do. By focusing on the colossal disaster that will take place if you ask for the business (if only in your imagination), you shut down and stop doing the important incremental things that will lead to your ultimate success. Act your way to confidence by behaving confidently. To appear confident:

- Smile. Why did you pay for all that expensive dental work if you weren't going to leverage your choppers? Besides, you're well prepared with witty and pithy comments that will set a friendly and relaxed mood. If you're there to sell as an act of compassion, which we hope you are, why wouldn't you smile? Smiling is a nonverbal way to ask for the business. If ever you doubt the power of a smile just remember how the way other people smiling at you relaxes your otherwise frantic nerves.
- Look your prospect in the eye. This is where you'll get that all-important feedback about how well you're making your case. Looking away timidly while hoping your customer is looking at you is the same kind of crap shoot as hoping he or she will interrupt you when it's time to close. Spend less time pointing at graphs and charts and more time connecting. As long as you're connected, you'll be confident. It's when you're not connected with eye contact that your fertile imagination will begin to catastrophize the outcome.
- Wear your best for them. If you mean business, dress like you mean business. It has been said that clothes make the person. The right clothes will certainly make the person feel better. Wearing sharp clothing that fits into your *i*-customers' cultures is a tribute and act of respect that will make them feel comfort-

able. One of the reasons we have a problem with the concept of business casual is, "When is the right time to throttle back and be casual about business?" Dressing more casually than a current or prospective customer can send the message that you don't take your relationship all that seriously.

- Wear your best for you. If you want your current and prospective customers to take you seriously you need to appear as if you're serious. You also want to appear as if you're successful. Nobody wants to work with a loser. Even if you feel like a loser on any given day you can deliberately put on the uniform of a successful person, which will make it much easier to play that part. Again, act your way out of doubt and uncertainty. There's nothing to stop you from looking like a million bucks, even if you feel like 50 bucks Canadian.

- Stay calm. Breathe. Relax. If you haven't properly prepared, this may be difficult. Do your homework. Remember what it felt like to be called on for an answer by your grammar-school teacher when you hadn't read the assignment? Why in creation would you go to all the trouble to meet with a current or prospective client and not be prepared? Deliberately breathing deeply and regularly will make you calm and relaxed. Not being prepared when the curtain goes up and it's time for you to ask for the business will make you stop breathing. You do the math.

- Speak with strength in your voice. No begging. No whining. Keep it real. No matter how you're feeling inside, remember that your current or prospective customers will appreciate you speaking clearly and loud enough for them to hear without constantly leaning forward, cupping their palms behind their ears, and saying, "What?" Your nervousness, as it can reveal itself through mumbling, speaking too softly, or not having a well-rehearsed, comprehensive pitch will sink your presentation every time.

Confidence is more important than experience. Great salespeople have the ability to transfer their urgency and the importance of their mission to their customers. You should have no problem creating urgency and motivation in yourself. If you can't do the deliberate and intentional things necessary to gain and maintain confidence, your chances of getting what you want out of life are practically nil. At the very least they are left to the fortunes of the unknown, blowing around like leaves in a storm. Share your confidence with your customers. Of all the acts of compassion associated with selling, that's at the top of the list.

LET GO OF THE OUTCOME

There is a difference between urgency and desperation. When salespeople operate out of desperation it weakens their position. Asking for the order is difficult enough without giving your *i*-customer an opportunity to disconnect. Everything you deliver with confidence, even the appearance of confidence, stands a good chance of addressing your current or prospective customers' problems. Why should people trust you to help solve their problems if you look like a walking passel of problems?

Being obsessed with whether your *i*-customer will blow you out of the water when you ask for the business will block you from doing the very things that will lead to a successful close. Obsessing over something out in the future, something you can't control, can make it nearly impossible to get the sale. Instead of wasting your focus and energy worrying about what might or might not happen, keep participating, asking, and doing those intentional incremental activities that build a platform for success.

Meanwhile, lower your level of attachment to the outcome. Don't try to drag your *i*-customers there kicking and screaming. Work toward the outcome you desire by taking the proper steps, one at a time. Lowering your attachment is different than no attachment. Of course you want your customer to say "Yes." But at the same time, if you're desperately obsessed with making the sale it will alter the way you ask. Focusing only on the outcome is like a basketball player trying to play a game by focusing on the scoreboard instead of the hoop. You're not shooting at the scoreboard, except perhaps rhetorically.

When your attention is on the scoreboard it's difficult to play the game. Do your homework, connect with your customer, make a great presentation, ask early and often as if you expect to make the sale, and let go of your attachment to the outcome. A line from Bob

Dylan's 1965 song, "Like a Rolling Stone," captures the thought— "When you ain't got nothin' you got nothin' to lose." Ask more and attach less.

Many A-type personalities spend their entire lives intensely participating, yet attached to the outcome of everything they do. They're like a heart attack waiting to happen. There are others who don't participate at all and have no attachment to the outcome. We call that resignation or indifference—the walking dead. Worse yet (a fate worse than death) is the person with low or no participation while at the same time maintaining a high level of attachment to the results. That's yet another definition of insanity.

People who don't participate and complain because they never get results are world-class complainers. They whine about not winning the lottery even though they never bought a ticket. Their ship will never come in because they never sent one out. Ships that never sail can never return with anything in the cargo hold. Like the lyrics of the song written by David Heuser in 2002 (based on the old hillbilly philosophy) imply, "How can I miss you when you won't go away?" Let go of your obsession with outcomes and you won't miss it.

THE SECRET TO CLOSING

The secret to closing the sale is there is no secret to closing the sale. No magic. It takes skill, perseverance, and a passion to help others. Closing is really about gaining agreement with your customer. Gaining agreement sounds much nicer and less manipulative than closing. In our experience the average salesperson closes 1 out of 10 customers. If you're one of those people you're working for free 90 percent of the time. It's common sense that you need to become more efficient at drawing a straight line between contacting current and prospective customers and closing.

All the preparation and planning, all the time spent connecting with your customers, all the needs assessments, and all the time spent presenting and prospecting are all wasted without a closed sale. Yes, much of selling is a numbers game, but we'd rather see you take a much more studied and surgical approach to gaining agreement from your customers than simply throwing what you've got up against enough walls until it sticks once or twice. When you imagine someone strictly taking the 'run it up the flagpole and see if anyone salutes' approach you start to wonder who needs the *i* in front of his or her name.

That's a lot of effort for no gain. Then, to add insult to injury, you hesitate to ask for the business. You've got to be kidding. Asking early and often is one of the surest ways to improve that closing ratio. Improving your closing ratio increases the payback for the time and effort you're expending. It all makes so much sense that it's a wonder we don't naturally become more eager with our asking—except for that pesky rejection thing. Fear is a powerful motivator. Putting it all in perspective, it's a wonder that we naturally avoid asking for the business when we could be gaining so much from the question.

In our experience in dealing with sales professionals it seems as if 50 percent of all presentations end without asking for the order. Many salespeople end their presentation by summarizing. Then they recap. Then they summarize again. Then they recap the recap. Suddenly we're back in that familiar place again, avoiding rejection by never asking for anything. As we said before, some sales are unilaterally closed by the customers. They listen to what you have to say, compare your product to others that are offering the same, and make a decision to purchase, or not, based on those facts as they perceive them. Lucky you. The biggest danger in this stroke of luck is salespeople fooling themselves into thinking they got the sale thanks to their superior selling skills. Can you spell i-d-i-o-t?

Closing by gaining agreement from your current or prospective customers is a natural last step in the sequence if you've done a good job on the prior steps. Keep in mind that your competition goes to bed every night plotting and scheming about ways to get your customers. There is very little margin for error. Your urgency is real, although it's always best to approach selling systematically, methodically, deliberately, and with the tremendous preparation we keep harping about.

THE ABCs OF LISTENING

We said earlier that you can make a fortune by doing a lot more listening and a lot less talking. If you've done a good job listening you bring it home when you ask for the business. Present your solution, ask for the order, and listen again to their response. If you're still a little fuzzy about listening, here are some tips:

- Shut up
- Keep quiet
- Don't talk

Any way you turn the phrase, it seems simple enough. Yet, you don't want to sit across from your *i*-customer and stare at one another in silence. Engage your current or prospective customers as we've discussed, by asking them how they see your product helping them solve problems. The smiles, the eye contact, the energized listening will draw the information out of them. The answers will flow out of their mouths, not yours. Once you see the sparkle in their eyes, stop selling and ask for the order. Just because they came to the realization that your product is what they need, don't overstay your welcome trying to convince them that it was all your idea.

Who cares? Don't let the flame of your customer's decision go out before you have a signature. By continuing to flap your gums long past the point of closing you're throwing a wet blanket over their flame. Bye-bye sale. Constantly reassure your customers that you're hearing what they're saying. Convey that you know what their most important issues are because you learned it from them, whether that's true or not. You can do this by reflecting their thoughts and comments back to them. They won't feel listened to, heard, or understood if you're busy ramming your impression and/or interpretation of their issues down their throats.

If you really know what they do, how they do it, when and where they do it, and why they do it the way they do—simply show them how your product or service can help them do it faster, better, and cheaper. Solve the problem they describe to you, not the one you imagine they have. As soon as they've articulated what they need, it's time for a trial close:

"If I can get you from where you are to where you want to be, is there anything preventing us from getting started right now?"

"I'd like to go over two options that may well bring an immediate solution to the most important challenge you mentioned."

"Based on everything you just shared with me can I share what I think would be a good next step?"

If they say no to that question you can be fairly certain that you haven't convinced them that you've been listening. If they say yes, get your contract or sales agreement out, stop telling, stop selling, and start writing. You cannot be complacent about asking for the order. Complacency is the first sign of indifference and it's your indifference to asking for the order that opens, and keeps opening, the window of opportunity for your *i*-customer to disconnect. Every disconnect you engineer with your *i*-customers is an opportunity for your competition to connect with them. Don't be your own worst enemy.

There is only one way you'll know if you've done a good job, addressed the right solution, and gained your customers' trust and confidence. They will ask, "Where do I sign?" Or, as Roger DiSilvestro put it, "Is there any limit to the amount of money we can spend with your company?" If your customer isn't ready to move ahead it's probably because there are objections and concerns, spoken or unspoken, that haven't yet been addressed. If there are it's probably because you haven't been listening well enough.

His or her silence and hesitancy to move forward will be your cue that you are going to have to make another pass and dig in a little deeper to overcome his or her objections and concerns. You will need to use your active listening skills here to discover what those concerns are. Don't give up. You're just preparing to ask for the order again. A "No" from your customer at this stage might just be the beginning, not the end.

MORE LESSONS FROM CHILDREN

Take another lesson from the greatest salespeople in the world: kids. They have no compunction whatsoever about asking for what they want. Have you ever noticed that kids don't summarize or recap? They move directly to the close by asking for what they want. Kids are less fazed by the word "No" than adults. If the child is young enough, the word "No" doesn't even seem to register, much less derail the childhood drive for gratification.

The question is not whether kids will ask for what they want. The question is, "Will kids ever stop asking for what they want?" Kids are the most relentless askers on the face of the planet. They came by those skills naturally. So did you. Kids didn't learn how to ask for what they want in a seminar. To children, closing skills and asking for what they want are as easy as breathing in and breathing out.

We've heard it argued that there is no such thing as a born salesperson. We disagree. It's true enough that selling skills can be taught and refined through mentoring, observation, study, and practice. But it's not as if we start without selling skills and acquire them over time. Doctors and nurses in delivery rooms don't hold up newly born infants and remark what a beautiful baby salesperson has just been born. But they might as well.

Babies are born ready to sell, with all the skills and natural abilities required to get everything they ever dreamed of. For most people, however, somewhere between the labor room and the conference room the basic skill for getting what they really want, which is asking, was lost or unlearned. Kids are born with a Gretzky-like intuition that although you don't always get what you ask for, you seldom if ever get what you don't ask for.

Unlike adults, kids expect to win over the customer. Kids don't start out fearing rejection. When adults say "No," kids merely figure we've made a mistake and they're patient and tolerant enough to provide us whatever time we need to rethink our answer, as long as it's immediately. On really major requests, like a pony, they might give us overnight before they remind us that they're waiting patiently for the correct answer. Kids are highly skilled at applying the five "whys" interrogation. But when a kid gets the answer he or she wants, the selling stops instantly.

Kids not only ask for what they want, they make totally unreasonable requests. People who make reasonable requests usually experience reasonable results. Kids don't edit their requests, they just ask and ask and keep asking. We asked a group of 7- to 9-year-olds how many times they had to ask their parents for something before they got what they wanted. The answers were—7 or 8 times. The thought of asking that many times and letting attrition do its work didn't trouble them at all. A clever, imaginative, and relentless request is the world's most powerful and neglected secret to success.

PERSONALITY-BASED ASKING

The same principle of asking for the order applies to our friends—the Machiavellians, sadists, masochists, paranoids, Greek gods, buddies, and decently good folks. Asking is a universal technique for cuing customers that it's time to buy. The booth is open, so to speak. The machine is ready to vend. Whatever. With any of these personality types, ask or ye shall not receive. The difference for each one, of course, is how you ask.

Ask the Machiavellian

It's not a good idea to be bossy with a Machiavellian. The disparity of power between you is important, not for the mere sake of having power, but for what the Machiavellian can do with it. Specifically, take you or anybody else out who gets in the Machiavellian's way. The Machiavellian would rather not be bothered taking people out because it slows down the fast track to the top. Ask the Machiavellian how he or she sees your product helping to achieve or even accelerate the achievement of his or her career agenda. At the first sign that he or she sees some potential synergy, ask how soon you can get started. The Machiavellian will say, "Yesterday."

Ask the Sadist

There are similarities in how you deal with sadists and Machiavellians, as well as distinct differences. As with the Machiavellian, the disparity of power between you and the sadist is important, not for the mere sake of having power, but for what the sadist can do with it. Specifically, punish you or anybody else within reach. Refer to your product as a tool to increase the sadist's power and influence, without getting into gory details. Again, as soon as there is a glimmer of recognition and excitement in the sadist's eyes, move to the close. Ask how quickly he or she would like to start seeing results. What exactly those results look like is none of your business, nor do you want to be hanging around to see them lest they involve you. But asking soon with a sadist will likely eliminate the need to ask often.

Ask the Masochist

The disparity of power between you is again important, not that the masochist wants power. He or she prefers that you keep it and use it in some nefarious way. Like we mentioned in earlier chapters, if your product will make life better for those around the masochist, either personally or professionally, the masochist will find comfort in suffering by comparison. Although you don't want to contribute to someone's life becoming a colossal disaster you can help everyone around that person. That's the virtuous move. How the masochist wants to frame the comparison is beyond your control, but not beyond usefulness to you. As in the case of the Machiavellian and the sadist, the masochist won't want to drag his or her feet when you ask how quickly he or she wants to begin feeling the effects of your transaction.

Ask the Paranoid

The disparity of power between you and the paranoid is not a big issue. The only thing the paranoid person would do with more power is to expose the conspiracy to take him or her down. Move quickly to the close and ask for the order because the sooner the benefits of your product are realized the sooner the true conspirators will be drawn out and exposed, or so you might want to intimate. It's kind of a twisted approach, but you're dealing with a twisted mind. If your paranoid current or prospective customers think that your product can move them toward a more solid foundation, one that is less vulnerable to sabotage, they will gladly give you their business and not allow any grass to grow under their feet in the process. If a paranoid balks or hesitates at all it's because he or she isn't sure whether or not you can be trusted.

Ask the Greek God or Goddess

If ever there was a time when it is about the customer, insane or not, this is it. You don't ask small-*g* gods. You beseech them. Talk about a disparity of power. Don't even pretend you're on the same playing field with these guys. You might be intellectually and morally superior in every way, but that's not how they see it. As with any customer, it's about how they see it, not how you see it. Your product must be presented in such a way as to enhance their self-deified status. We've already covered that ground. But asking if you can begin the process of building their kingdoms is sure to elicit a positive response. In other words, are they going to say "No?" In case you haven't detected the pattern here, asking for the order from anyone, whatever form your question takes, must clearly imply, "How soon can I begin giving you exactly what you want and need?"

Ask Your Best Buddy

"The sooner we conclude this deal," you chirp, "the sooner I'll be back to see if you want another." If your customer's a big enough idiot to go for that, you've hit the lottery, albeit a small one. It's much more likely that your best-buddy *i*-customer will be smart enough to know that the way to keep you around is to postpone a decision, delay, hesitate, um-m-m and ah-h-h, hem and haw. Let him or her know that you've only been allotted so much time to pursue any given account. If he or she can't pull the trigger you're under orders to seek greener pastures. But, and it's a big one, if he or she wants to move to the contract you have carte blanche to spend all the time they want (depending upon the size of the order, of course). And you have permission to come back soon. That'll get your buddy moving.

Ask the Decent Soul

No games here. Not even fooling around like we do with the Machiavellian, sadist, masochist, paranoid, and buddy customers. The decent soul wants it straight much in the same way you do. CECO with the decent soul. Give him or her credit for being able to make up his or her mind. If the decent soul hesitates it's probably not because you haven't catered to his or her eccentricities. It's probably because he or she has lingering, legitimate concerns that you have yet to address. The refreshing thing about selling to decent souls is that your highly refined selling skills all come into play and pay dividends the way they are designed to work. You just need to stick by your active listening, provide information honestly and concisely in response to his or her curiosity, and ask, ask, ask.

CHAPTER SIX SUMMARY

Even though professional salespeople are trained to ask for the order, only about half of them do, about half the time. We said that only an idiot salesperson would leave it up to the customer to beg to buy. Yet that's what happens much too often. Can we all be idiots? Not really. But we are creatures in search of comfort. Being told "No" is uncomfortable. The answer is to ask for the order as part of a well-planned and orchestrated strategy to gain agreement from the customer piece-by-piece. Some of the finer elements of asking for the order include:

- Be the first to say "Please": If you're really too bashful to ask for the order because that opens up the possibility for the customer to say "No," do you really expect an idiot customer to come to your rescue by saying "Please?" Ask early how the customer can visualize your product helping him or her solve problems or achieve greater results. If he or she has a clear image ask how soon you can begin.

- Asking is an action verb: Nothing ventured, nothing gained. Be led by your own interpretation of the Gretzkyism about missing all the shots you don't take, as long as it leads you to the inescapable conclusion that you'll probably miss all the shots you don't take. You can be lucky some of the time. But living for those rare exceptions won't put you in a newer car or fatten up your kids.

- Don't work for free 90 percent of the time: Refining and enhancing your professional selling skills will make the difference between how much of your investment or time, energy, and resources you waste versus how much you cash in on. You wouldn't intentionally set out to waste 90 percent of your time. More specifically, you wouldn't intentionally give up 90 percent of your income unless you intend to leave the land of the capitalists and devote your life to serving the world's needy. Nothing wrong with that. But why pretend to be a sales professional on a Peace Corps salary?

- Use humor to loosen up: As Athlon Sports Publishing CEO and sales guru Roger DiSilvestro shared with us, "Blow them away with something funny." The healing and calming properties of humor will bring a breath of fresh air to your customers and put your own nerves at ease at the same time. Use it deliberately, wisely, and prudently. Some sales people think they need to tell a tired or dirty joke to break the ice. We don't agree with either. Lame humor is just that; lame. Off-color humor is offensive. Save it for your cigar-smoking poker buddies—if you have any cigar-smoking poker buddies. Rehearse how to take the environment you and your current or prospective customers are operating in, twist the lens on it, and find some genuine humor—at your expense, not theirs.

• Stay out of the outcomes: You can't control the big picture. The best you can hope for is to handle the little things that make up the big picture, and not all of those are under your control. Think of it as putting together a puzzle. When you're staring at a box full of little pieces you know what the finished product will look like by looking at the cover, but getting there will take patience and a determined approach. Selling is more like playing the *Wheel of Fortune* on TV. You don't need to assemble all the clues before you leap to the answer. But you need enough of them in place. You wouldn't do well guessing the answer with no letters showing. As soon as it appears that you and your customer have enough mutual understanding, take your shot. Ask for the order. The outcome will fall together fast enough.

• Watch children sell circles around you: Children make it clear how much they want what they want. However, they're clever enough to frame it in how it will bring benefits to everyone. Asking for the proverbial pony, a kid will generously offer to let you ride it after he or she has gone to bed. Wouldn't that be fun? To hear the kid tell it, the camping trip or the cross-country drive to Disneyland Resort or MGM Studios will be the thrill of your lifetime, not just theirs. You know what? Sometimes they're right. Given your skills and abilities as a sales professional, ask for the order, baby, 'cause chances are good that you're right, too. Remember, asking for the business is the natural conclusion to your pitch, not the final conflict.

Have you noticed that we're not throwing around the term "idiot" as much as we were earlier? By now it should be painfully clear that the troubles you face increasing sales volume and margin are not as much about idiot customers as they are about you. That's where your focus should be. Stop wasting your time by putting them down and start investing your precious time and energy in building yourself up. Maybe your customers are colossal morons. If they are there's nothing you can do to change them. But you can make enormous strides in how effective you are as a sales professional. We continue in Step Seven with Circling Around and Making Another Pass.

7

STEP SEVEN: CIRCLE AROUND AND MAKE ANOTHER PASS

Okay, you might get shot down. It happens. But more often than not, you haven't crashed and burned. You simply haven't adequately addressed the idiot's objections yet. If you think you have addressed all objections and your customer is not buying simply because he's an idiot, then look in a mirror. You've probably also been listening too much to your inner idiot. Salespeople who struggle to make ends meet or simply fall short of their goals are usually better at generating objections than overcoming them. Get your own objections out of the way before you can address your customer's objections.

At every bump in the road great salespeople say, "The sale begins now." You might think there's a contradiction there. Didn't I just get shot down? Didn't the sale just end? No. A smarter sales professional is about to begin a new sale. Your *i*-customers might be idiots, but they're customers first. Regardless of their mental capacities, they have what you want. The question thus becomes, "Whose inner idiot will prevail?" If you got shot down the first time it's obvious who's prevailing . . . for the moment.

Remember that people don't make decisions in confusion. Check in to see if you muddied the waters and forgot to clear them up again. Idiot salespeople wait for the idiots across the desk to state the issues blocking them from saying "Yes." That's the clueless leading the clueless. Sometimes the one doing the selling clumsily creates confusion and then hopes the customer will clear it up. It's more likely that the customer will clear out the salesperson. If the customer is stalling, you need to diagnose where you slipped up and remedy the situation quickly, because your 30-minute sales appointment just became a 7-minute sales appointment.

GET OUT THERE AND FAIL

Never fear. Failing the first time, even the second or third, places you in good company. Our friend Danny Cox, in his aforementioned book, *Leadership When the Heat's On,* lists some early-game losers that we wouldn't mind being associated with:

1. He was labeled unsociable and mentally slow. He didn't start talking until he was 4 years old. His own father said that he wasn't normal and wouldn't amount to anything. He was eventually expelled from school.
2. The man entered the conflict a captain and was busted down to private. He left the military and became a farm laborer. His military and civilian careers were stuck in reverse.
3. This person's childhood voice teacher said that that he had no vocal talent at all.
4. This man's employers told him that he didn't have enough sense to wait on customers. He was relegated to stocking shelves at the dry goods store where he worked until the age of 21.
5. The editor of the newspaper where he worked accused him of being "void of creativity" and fired him, citing "lack of good ideas."
6. Consistently at the bottom of the class, this man's teachers said he was too stupid to learn anything. He was finally educated at the knee of his patient mother.

7. Her parents received a letter from the acting school where she was a student explaining that her teachers felt she had no talent and recommended that the parents waste no more money on the child's theatrical training. She failed at audition after audition and struggled to overcome a crippling disease. She didn't walk for 2 years. Finally, at age 40 she landed her first noteworthy acting role.

8. He played varsity basketball for Laney High School in Wilmington, North Carolina until he was cut from the team. Instead of giving up, he practiced on his own hour after hour, imagining the list in the locker room without his name on it. His hard work eventually earned him back his spot on the roster.

It's pretty transparent where we're going with this. You've no doubt heard such paradoxical descriptions before. We could list millions of examples depicting how people's lives appeared to be hopeless only to be redeemed later. Yet, when we're shot down by a current or prospective customer we instinctively consider it hopeless. We quickly overcome that feeling with rational thinking, as you do, but the gut reaction is despair. So, it never hurts to remind ourselves that we've lived through worse and survived to fight another day. Oh, you're probably wondering who those losers are in the previous list. Let's see:

1. Mentally slow and expelled from school—Albert Einstein
2. A leadership failure in the military-turned-farm laborer—Abraham Lincoln
3. The boy with no vocal talent—Enrico Caruso
4. Too dumb to wait on customers—F. W. Woolworth
5. Void of creativity with no good ideas—Walt Disney
6. Too stupid to learn anything—Thomas A. Edison
7. No theatrical talent—Lucille Ball
8. Cut from the basketball team—Michael Jordan

LEARN TO LOVE THE LESSONS

Successful people have learned to fail their way to success. While they may not particularly enjoy their failures they recognize them as an unavoidable experience on their journey to victory. More than merely being unavoidable, successful people have learned that disappointments and setbacks are opportunities to learn. If you're properly motivated the more you learn the more you'll earn. One big lesson to learn is that disappointment won't kill you.

Television talk show host Sally Jesse Raphael, according to her authorized television biography, couldn't pay her credit card bills for 26 years. During that period she moved 25 times looking for work, was fired 18 times, and never earned more than $22,000 a year. Worse yet, there were times when she lived on food stamps and slept in her car.

At what point would you have told her to give it up? When you get right down to it there is no such thing as failure. There are only results—some more successful than others. Failure means you've reached the end of the line and that success is not possible. The only time that happens is when you quit. Quitting is final. Continued attempts with commitment and perseverance can always be turned into success. For the most successful people we know, disappointments and setbacks barely break their strides. To them every setback is an opportunity. Putting setbacks and disappointments into proper perspective is a learned skill. Proficiency at any skill requires time, effort, and discipline, and the willingness to persevere through whatever difficulties may arise.

TURNAROUND QUESTIONS

Pilots recalibrate their flight instruments before every flight. When's the last time you recalibrated your navigational equipment? Most of the cockpit instruments the pilot checks are just fine. However, some are dependent on changing conditions. An altimeter, for example, measures barometric pressure. Temperature and moisture in the air change constantly. So the altimeter is adjusted not only before each flight, but throughout each flight.

What conditions are changing constantly in your professional environment versus the ones that remain fairly static or stable? Market conditions? Your customers' moods? The competition? How faithfully have you recalibrated your navigational instruments to accommodate the conditions you're currently facing? This means making sure your instruments read the conditions properly and guide you accurately toward your desired destination. You recalibrate by asking the right questions—questions that will help you turn around undesirable outcomes. If you aren't getting the results you want or have been discouraged by disappointments or setbacks, ask yourself these questions:

- Do I have an unrealistic timetable? Maybe you expect to skip steps and succeed on a grand scale immediately. That means you're back in the outcomes business. Success is usually achieved by climbing one step at a time. So be patient with yourself and resist the temptation to compare your progress to that of anyone else. People who are extremely successful probably don't get that way overnight. Compete only against yourself and you can only win. The question is, "How big?"
- Am I truly committed? Do you have a burning desire to achieve your goal? It's essential that you be willing to do whatever it takes (within legal and ethical bounds, of course) and that you banish any thought of giving up before you accomplish your objective. If you haven't been willing to do whatever it takes in the past, what makes you think it will be any different in the future? If something is blocking you before you finished the race, find out what it is and unblock yourself.
- Do I have too many discouraging influences? Unsuccessful results can be frustrating. That's why we need to surround ourselves with those who support and believe in us. If you hang around with negative people who are highly critical or who are doing very little in their own lives, your energy and enthusiasm will be drained. Negative people tend to discourage rather than encourage your success. Hang out with positive, powerful people—or at least powerfully positive people.
- Am I preparing to succeed? Success in any endeavor requires thorough preparation. Are you taking steps to learn everything you can about accomplishing your goal? This means reading books, listening to tapes, taking courses, and networking with highly successful people in your field. It might mean finding a mentor or getting a coach to work with you. Successful individuals are always sharpening their skills. Get a little better every day.

- Am I truly willing to fall short? Face it, it's going to happen. You will encounter more defeats than victories. The goal is to win the war despite your battle record. Look disappointment squarely in the face and see it as a natural part of the success process. Then and only then will it lose its power to control you and block you from trying again and again.
- Am I talking to the person who has the authority to say yes to my request? Maybe I need to circle around and land somewhere else. Only an idiot would squander precious selling time presenting to someone who needs the approval of another party to buy. One of your first questions should have been "If you decide this product is right for your company . . . if this house or car is right for your family (whatever) do you have the authority to make a commitment to purchase it?" If you don't get that qualifying issue resolved early you'll be circling the airport for a long time.

It's been said a thousand times in a thousand ways: It's not how many times you fall down—it's how many times you get up. You might fall so often as to conclude that you're in the falling business. We'd prefer you to say that you're in the getting up business. The truth is that when you are no longer afraid to fall now and then you're well on your way to success. Welcome disappointment as an un-avoidable-yet-vital component in the quest to achieve your goals. Your disappointments are learning experiences that point to the adjustments you must make. Never try to hide from disappointment. Hiding guarantees that you'll take virtually no risks and will achieve very little. The kind of lifestyle you want for yourself and your family won't be achieved by playing it safe all the time. Risk more.

You won't close every sale. That's why you know how to circle back, not fly off into oblivion. You won't make money on every investment. Life is a series of wins and losses, even for the most successful. If you make it your business to learn from every defeat and stay focused on the end result you want to attain, disappointment will eventually lead you to success—one step at a time. If you want to get there faster, stay focused like a laser beam on the process that leads to your desired end result.

We say that if you can't or are unwilling to hear the word "No," you may never hear a "Yes." If you are someone who has a hard time hearing someone say "No," it will affect the type of questions you ask. You will only ask safe questions, which can only be answered with "Yes." A very safe selling career will be your fate. So will the skinny children and the old car. No rejection, no objections, and no results of any magnitude. You will also have a problem saying "No" to others. People who over-commit and underachieve frustrate everyone around them—not the least of which is them. If they're in such denial as to their abilities and accomplishments that they don't frustrate themselves, the rest of us will find dealing with them that much more frustrating.

One of the most profound differences between high performers and low performers is their tolerance of the word "No." Like kids, great salespeople have a filter over their ears. When someone says "No," to a kid it enters their filter and they hear "Maybe," "Not just yet," or "Come back later." Great salespeople never lost that filter over their ears. Or they learned to reinstall it. They also have a short memory. They don't dwell on the "No." They gather themselves and prepare to circle around and make another pass at asking for the order.

Some say that selling never really begins until the customer says "No," or presents an objection. This is where you must go on offense, not defense. The old style of selling taught that you were to present your product and/or service, ask for the order, wait for the objection, and then counter or overcome it. That's a little too passive for us. There is a proverb that says, "The man who sits on a stump waiting for a roasted chicken to fly into his open mouth will wait a long time."

OBJECTIONS

The only objections that you can't handle are the ones you don't hear. Some salespeople spend their entire career dodging objections by simply not hearing them. Top salespeople are not only good at overcoming objections, they're masters at generating objections. They know that satisfying their customers' real concerns and objections is the path to completing their sale. They don't stop the first time their customer says "No."

When your current or prospective customers raise objections they are really presenting a gesture of good faith. By taking the time to share their real concerns or problems with you they're passing along more important information that includes key facts on how your product and/or presentation needs to be adapted in order to meet their needs. In our experience it seems as though 80 percent of customers have the same objections. You must be willing and able to offer solutions and explain benefits to their satisfaction before you can move on.

You must be able to distinguish between your customers' real concerns versus their smokescreens before giving answers or asking for the order again. You must hear what isn't being said as you listen to what is being said. Treat objections like questions, as if your customer is still confused and requires more clarity. Remember that every objection indicates interest in your product.

What Objections Really Are

- An unanswered question in disguise: Sometimes your current or prospective customers want to know something but aren't quite sure how to ask. Maybe they're not the proficient, professional askers you are. So they imitate what they've seen other people do to salespeople. They object.
- A buying signal: Your customers are ready to pull the trigger, but want some last-minute reassurance that they're not making a mistake. Perhaps your customers are ready to sign the deal, but want to test your resolve one last time to see if you have the spine to be their supplier.
- Selling opportunity: When customers raise an objection they may be saying, "I really like what you're selling and I'm wondering if I shouldn't buy more of it." In this case, the objection starts or restarts the closing process. We've often seen someone who is protesting suddenly buy more than we had originally expected.
- May just be a statement: Just as some customers don't really know how to formulate a question, some of your current or prospective customers might not know how to articulate a statement to express how they feel. Listen carefully. There may not actually be an objection in their objection.

- A chance to create a distinction: If your customer says, "The ACME Company has the same thing," he or she might not have any intention of buying from the moron who sells for the ACME Company. Your customer just wants to make sure you're not a moron and is giving you a chance to prove yourself.

Why Salespeople Dodge Objections

- They're unprepared: Many sales professionals haven't come to believe in the power of preparation. It's as if they're saying, "Yeah, I'll sell for a living. But only if it's easy. I have the tools and the knowledge to do this really well, but practicing is boring. When I get in front of the customer, it'll be Showtime."
- Lack of confidence: Self-esteem issues can be a real downfall for someone in sales. But low self-esteem doesn't need to cripple a salesperson any more than cancer crippled Lance Armstrong. It simply becomes another challenge to be acknowledged and dealt with. This too can be overcome.
- Poor selling skills: Some people in sales just don't think they should study and practice to sharpen their skills. To them sales should happen naturally or not at all. They only want to deal with that rare customer who says, "I've been waiting for you to call." They are trying to live in the exception column.
- Lack of product knowledge: Some salespeople think to themselves, "If customers want what I'm selling they'll buy. If not, all the information in the world won't matter. Providing a secure, upscale lifestyle for my family just isn't worth spending time at home or on weekends adding to my product knowledge."
- Don't believe in the product: "I need to do something for a living," thinks the melancholy salesperson. "I might as well sell this." The problem is that the salesperson didn't choose the product or company based on their merits. If selling is truly an act of compassion you must believe that your product is helping someone.

How to Resolve Objections

- Be curious and ask clarifying questions: If you truly believe in your product and the company you represent, you need to find out which parts of the customer-product connection are disconnected, or failed to connect in the first place. Use skilled, surgical questions to reveal the true issues and where the confusion is, so you can address them.

- Ask if the objection is your customer's primary concern: You need to determine quickly if your customer is being completely forthcoming about why he or she is pushing back. You don't want to waste precious time and energy emptying your chamber on a target other than the primary target.

- Offer solutions: Don't deny that your customer's concerns are legitimate, even if you feel they're ridiculous. Say, "You raise a legitimate concern, Mr. (or Ms.) So-and-So." Having said that, he or she will accept what you're about to say because he or she feels listened to and respected.

- Gain agreement: "Would you agree that . . . ?" By pointing out how much common ground you share with your customers you are minimizing the potential magnitude of dissonance and points of contradiction. As long as your customers think they'll be mostly happy with their decision, they'll buy.

- Back to asking for the order: If at first you don't succeed, try again. Maybe your customer is simply too proud to buy on the first close. He or she might feel that a second, third, or fourth close will make you more appreciative of their business. Don't let an objection lead you far from another close attempt.

You will close the sale when your customer perceives and believes that the value and benefits of your product outweigh the value of the money you are asking him or her to dish out. Stay focused on the things that matter most. Value, solutions, and benefits—everything else is just fluff. If your customer hasn't said "Yes," he or she is still not clear about the big three: value, solutions, and benefits of your product and/or service. He or she is still confused. As we mentioned in Chapter Three and reminded you earlier in this chapter, customers will only make a purchase out of clarity. They will never feel comfortable purchasing out of confusion.

Buyer's remorse and cancelled sales occur generally because the real issues, objections, and concerns of your customers were never satisfied. If you can successfully clear your customers' concerns and objections you gain a psychological advantage when you circle around to land the next time. Go right into another trial close and ask once more for the order.

Pay extra-close attention to your customer at this point. Too often, salespeople get so used to hearing the word "No," that when a customer says "Yes," they aren't prepared to proceed with the sale—worse yet, they just keep on talking the way we've described, and talk themselves right out of the sale. The customer may not say the word "Yes," but may be saying it with body language. Remember that communication is only 7 percent words and 93 percent other means of expression. Customers will show you if they're interested. So stay awake. You don't want to sleep through the "Yes," whether the word actually passes your customers' lips or not.

DON'T BE THE MONKEY

It's an unconscious motor reaction for current or prospective customers to balk at price. Weak and inexperienced salespeople therefore focus all of their time and energy on the selling price. It's a common monkey-see, monkey-do objection. Don't bite. A study done by Harvard Business School revealed that 94 percent of all sales are made on a nonprice basis. Only an idiot would spend all of his or her time selling price. There is always someone with a lower price. Besides, the price objection is usually not your customer's primary concern, anyway. It's just another pesky and aggravating smoke-screen.

Average salespeople sell features. Features are logical. But your customers' decision to purchase is not based on logic. It's emotion that moves customers from "Maybe" to "Yes." Top salespeople know that price is important and that features are nice—but they sell benefits, value, and solutions with emotional appeal.

In your attempt to use perseverance and to keep asking, remember that your current or prospective customers won't change their own minds from a "No" to a "Yes." They will opt to make a new decision based on new information if you open the door for them. Your customers make informed decisions, which means decisions informed by emotions—the greatest of which are comfort and confidence. Whatever information you're supplying, it must increase your customers' sense of comfort and confidence.

Don't sound like a broken record as you circle around and make another pass at your customers and ask for the order. Broken records don't provide new information. If your customers have not agreed to your original request, change your strategy. If you are digging holes in the wrong place, digging them deeper won't matter. The key to great selling is the ability to anticipate obstacles. You should never be caught offguard. A "No" from your current or prospective customers is just one of the obstacles to gaining the sale that you prepared for and fully expect to close. Don't be surprised. Your preparation gives you the ability to think on your feet. We're not suggesting at this point that you completely reverse your field and start whining until your customer agrees to purchase. However, don't be so in love with your tactics that you go down in flames.

MORE LESSONS FROM CHILDREN

Kids reject rejection. One of the reasons that kids keep asking in the face of hearing "No" is that they have a higher tolerance for the word than many adult salespeople. They don't get discouraged. They haven't yet learned that rejection is supposed to slow you down, hurt your feelings, and damage your self-esteem. Rejection is something that kids will allow to seep into their sensibilities later in life. Great salespeople, as well as kids, are very willing to hear the word "No" and keep on keeping on.

Kids change their strategies quickly and easily when they meet resistance to getting what they want. They don't know enough to be prudent in what they ask for. Prudence and restraint in asking is another thing learned as we get older. In their innocence kids ask for the impossible and unimaginable, and often succeed in getting what they ask for. If kids think that whining, crying, stomping their feet, or knocking over a lamp will help them in getting the attention required to get what they want, they will. They change their strategy on the fly. If they don't get the answers they want from Mom they circle around and ask Dad. If they don't get the results they want from him they make a run at Grandpa and Grandma. Kids will circle and come back at you as often as it takes.

PERSONALITY-BASED OBJECTIONS

The unique and sometimes eccentric personalities you must deal with out in the world can be complex and difficult to fully understand. Don't be too hard on yourself if you don't nail your target on the first pass. You might need to circle several times before you acquire the correct coordinates on this one or that one. However, the objections you hear from various personality types can be clues to identify which personality type you're dealing with. Addressing objections must be done in a personality-specific manner or you're likely to make matters worse.

The Machiavellian Objects

Don't be surprised to hear a Machiavellian say, "I don't see how that helps me." Duh. Machiavellians are all about themselves and their fast-track to the top. If you haven't been pitching how your product will get the Machiavellian into the executive suite and/or the mansion on the hill from the get-go, you've been whistling Dixie. If any objection comes out of the Machiavellian's mouth, regardless of what it is, it can only mean one thing. The big M doesn't think your product is a career catalyst. Circle around and this time remember what the Machiavellian lives for.

The Sadist Objects

If you have failed to position your product in such a way as to render the sadist in a more powerful position from which to pursue his or her nefarious agenda you've wasted everybody's time, and might deserve to be slapped around a little. No matter how the sadist's objection is worded, it's about the pain. The sadist might say, "I don't know if that price is going to fly with my CFO." Ignore the comment. The sadist is really saying, "I don't think that price is going to cause my CFO enough pain." If the sadist complains about price, say, "We can always double it." You might get your signature right there on the spot.

The Masochist Objects

The masochist might also present an objection based on price. The natural inclination would of course be to reduce the price and ease his or her pain. First of all, you don't lower anybody's price in response to the bogus price objection. Second of all, you double the price with the masochist just like you did with the sadist. The reason is different, however. With the latter you want to help cause pain to others. With the former you want to cause pain, period. If the masochist objects for any reason, he or she is really telling you that the deal you're offering doesn't hurt enough. To win over the masochist, circle back with a more punitive offer.

The Paranoid Objects

Any objection that passes the paranoid personality's lips means, I don't trust you. "It's too expensive," means, "I don't trust you." "It's not a good fit for our company," means, "I don't trust you." "It's a water-based product and we're an oil-based organization," means, "I don't trust you." Paranoids are difficult because it will be practically impossible for you to earn their trust. You can, however, circle back with a more appealing arrangement. Explain to the paranoid personality how your product, or working with you—better yet, how buying your product *and* working with you—will expose the conspiracy. He or she still might not trust you, but exposing the conspiracy is his or her greatest fantasy.

The Greek God or Goddess Objects

Objections coming down from Mount Olympus are probably procedural. Greek gods and goddesses are sticklers for protocol. "It's too expensive" can mean your offering was too cheap. "It costs too much" can mean your confession was unacceptable. "We can't afford it" can mean . . . oh, please . . . even small-*g* gods think they can afford anything. That's really a lame objection. However, it could mean that you looked at their faces instead of casting your gaze at their feet. Who knows? Whatever excuse they offer for not buying, when you circle around and come back at them, you had better be contrite. Speak only when you're spoken to, and don't forget the incense this time.

Your Best Buddy Objects

"It's too expensive," coming from your best buddy's mouth, can mean, "Please don't close yet, I'm still having fun." "It costs too much" can mean, "Please don't close yet, I'm still having fun." "We can't afford it" probably means, "Please don't close yet, I'm still having fun." As we advised before, threaten to leave. When you circle around say, "I can only offer this to you one more time. If you don't accept, I'm under orders to leave. But if you agree to buy, we can spend all afternoon working up the contract together. If we spend the afternoon working up the contract together, and then you back out," you threaten, "my boss says I can never come here again." She or he will probably not be able to resist the temptation. Whatever you're asking will be a small price to pay for your companionship. Besides, if it's a business-to-business sale, it's not his or her money anyway.

A Decent Soul Objects

When a decent soul says, "It's too expensive," money is truly an issue. It's time to circle back with creative financing, not a lower price. Or you could move up the volume chart where the per-unit price drops. He or she will be saving money over time. If a decent soul says, "I still don't understand how this is going to help us," he or she truly doesn't understand how your product is going to help. Circle back with clearer and more concise information to help your customer connect the dots. If a decent soul says, "Your product is made from beef by-products and our entire clientele is Hindu," thank the prospective customer, go back to the office, and snap rubber bands against your wrists for not doing your homework.

CHAPTER SEVEN SUMMARY

Just because you get knocked down doesn't mean you need to stay down. In fact, people watching you will probably be surprised and disappointed if they see you stay down. Remember what great sales-people say: "At every bump in the road, the selling begins again." We mentioned earlier how pilots and flight planners always load enough fuel for the plane to circle its destination or divert to another destination. Be prepared to do the same. If you aren't cleared to land on your first approach, circle around and approach again. The mantra Close Early and Close Often might mean taking a lot of approaches.

- Get out there and fail: You will suffer many minor defeats on your way to winning the war. Minor defeats are just that, however—minor. As long as you honor the incremental steps that lead to ultimate success you will transform minor defeats into major victories, and major victories will win the day. Allowing minor defeats to stop your effort is career suicide.

- Learn to love the lessons: Every objection your current or prospective customers place in your path is an opportunity to learn. Like we said, the more you learn the more you earn. As you circle around you become smarter with each pass. It's about learning: You never stop. Not only do the lessons you learn from this customer help close this sale, they will help you gain agreement with your next customer faster.

- Ask turnaround questions: Asking for the order is not the only asking you'll need to do. When your current or prospective customers offer objections you need to suddenly switch gears and become CSI: Sales Call. What really happened here? What's really going down? Of course those aren't questions, but they're the curiosity. Your skilled, surgical questions will quickly get to the essence of your customers' genuine concerns and distinguish them from their bogus complaints.

- Don't fall for the price objection: Unless someone is spending his or her own money price is probably not that big of a deal. Even if it is their own money, what remains most important is justifying the expenditure to someone with the power to punish them for it. You're giving your current or prospective customers all the ammunition they need to make their cases to those who hold them accountable. It's not about money as much as it's about justification and feeling good about the purchase later. Value, solutions, and benefits are the substance of feeling good about the decision to buy.

- Don't be afraid to hear "No": Be more like the kid you used to be. Reinstall those filters over your ears that removed the sting from the word "No." "No" filters don't block the word altogether, it just loses its power to stop you in your tracks. Take the word "No" and hear it for what it really means: "I don't understand," "I'm confused," or "I'm scared." When you hear the true meaning you'll understand the genuine concern your customer is voicing. Armed with that knowledge you can circle back and effectively address it.

How do you feel now? Beaten down? Deflated? Are you ready to pack up and crawl back into your car and head for your next sales visit? If so, then that is just what it was, a sales visit, which is very different from a sales call. Regardless of your feelings, this isn't the time to wave the white flag. It's time to hunker down and bring out your secret weapon. The next step is what separates the top salespeople from the average producers. Remember, if you keep doing what you have always done you'll get what you've always gotten. It's time to become a little more unpredictable. To achieve great results in your life, you have to come face to face with what you have been avoiding. Have you been avoiding becoming annoying?

8

Step Eight: Annoy Them a Little and Ask for the Business, Again

Asking questions is one of the most powerful tools a salesperson has at his or her disposal. But that's not enough. You must also learn the fine art of becoming pleasantly annoying. If your customer hesitated when you asked for the order the first time it's probably because you weren't sharp enough with your questioning or your listening. Get pleasantly unreasonable with your questions. Kids don't ask reasonable questions, and they'll always catch adults off balance sooner or later. No matter how hard we swear that a kid won't get the drop on us again, they will.

Kids understand that those who ask a lot get a lot. They have that Wayne Gretzky thing down pretty well—long before they ever know who Wayne Gretzky is. The more you shoot the more you score. If you watch a kid in a pee-wee basketball game dribble, dribble, and dribble, he or she is prouder of the ability to dribble than of scoring points. The same with passing. If a pee-wee basketball player passes the ball every time he or she touches it, and never shoots, it's safe to conclude that scoring is not his or her top priority. The kid's reason might be simple: It's hard to get the ball through the hoop. Passing and dribbling are easier. For adults, that's called losing focus.

You want to get a lot, don't you? Money, prestige, security, and comfort won't cascade into your life if you talk instead of sell, or if you visit your current or prospective customers without asking for the order. When you detect a sparkle in your customer's eye or in his or her voice, start shooting. You should be in your game plan long before you come into your current or prospective customer's presence.

If you've worked hard at addressing the customer's last real concerns, if you've circled around several times, there's only one way to find out if you've dug yourself out of the hole. Ask for the order again. If you've cleared up the confusion to his or her satisfaction, game over. If you've made the customer believe that he or she will feel good about his or her decision after the purchase, you're home free. Perhaps you weren't clear enough when you asked the first time and you simply need to be more direct. Whatever. Congratulations—you've reached a place of agreement with your customer. If only it always went that smoothly. If there is any hesitation left, your customer might invite you to come back and explain the product or service some more, which is to send you away empty-handed.

TEACHING THE CUSTOMER HOW TO BUY

After hearing "No" once or several times, your competition will usually make a beeline for the door. But not you. That's not how you do business. What we are asking you now is to be unreasonable with yourself and to stay just a little bit longer. This could be the tiebreaker in the deadlock. We believe this is the point where most salespeople bail out, and it is where you can begin to see results where up until now you haven't. Many people are comfortable with mediocrity. They feel okay in that "customer is thinking about it" zone. It's very familiar. The thought of succeeding in a big way is scary. It will be a big change, for one thing. So we tend to stay in our comfort zones.

We are asking you now to leave your comfort zone. We realize that's not easy for most people. People fear most what they don't understand and what is unknown. This is unknown territory for most salespeople. Turning up the burner under the success pot might make it boil. Things could get hot. Some salespeople actually ask for the order. Some even ask twice. But we're asking you to hang in there long enough to ask at least one more time. What you're doing is teaching your customer how to buy. Isn't that a nice thing to do?

Customers become conditioned to expect salespeople to give up after one or two attempted closes. Therefore they set their timers when salespeople come to call, and after some polite conversation they say "No," in whatever manner suits their mood or situation. They even expect to hear a second attempt to close—to which they are well prepared to say "No," again—with or without a lame excuse associated with it. Hope that your competition is as timid and bashful as we intimated a moment ago. That leaves the door open for you to get serious.

However, those salespersons who pack up and retreat after one or two failed closes have taught the customers that their refusals to buy work. By giving up, weak and ineffective salespeople have taught customers that they can win and win easily. You, on the other hand, have a different lesson to teach. When your current or prospective customers expect to shoo you away with one or two rejections they are confused when you circle back on them. Their initial confusion can give way to curiosity, for a while. Then they might get a little aggravated at your persistence. But they're learning how serious you are; serious about helping them.

In many training sessions we've had salespeople tell us this is overkill. We're suggesting that staying a little longer and asking a little more may not be your style, but if you are planning on producing results that exceed anything you've ever produced before, you must be willing to try things you've never tried before. To have more, you must be willing to become more. Don't buy into the copout that it's a numbers game and that if your customers don't go down with the first or second shot it's time to move on to the next number.

If you're that shallow and impatient you never believed that you were going to truly help them anyway. If you genuinely believe that selling is an act of compassion, you'll have the confidence and motivation to push back the boundaries of your comfort zone when needed. As business coach Paulette Sun says, "Using compassion is the difference between annoying and pleasantly annoying." Eventually your customer will learn to trust your sincerity and determination. That's the lesson you want to teach your customers, and you can't teach them that lesson if you cut and run. It's not exactly a "spare the rod and spoil the child" mentality. It is, however, a "show them that you mean business" mentality all the way.

FAILURE IS YOUR FRIEND

Earlier we spoke about failing yourself forward. All progress is preceded by small disappointments. A lack of disappointment in one's life often reveals a lack of effort or a personal policy of playing it safe. All we're talking about here is being a little more persistent than your competition. Okay, a lot more persistent. Often you outlast your competition more than outwork them. Hanging in there longer creates more opportunities for you to become lucky. Please understand that we believe luck is a choice. You put yourself in the path of luck or you don't. Being in your customers' offices or on the telephone with them or recently in their vicinity is like strapping yourself to the railroad track and waiting for the luck locomotive to roll by. Sooner or later it will, and you'll be in its path.

People don't ordinarily think that being hit by a train is a good thing. But if it's the luck locomotive, you want to be hit. The luck locomotive keeps no regular schedule. No human being knows when it will pass by. Most hope that they will coincidentally be crossing the track at the right time. But it's like the "can't win the lottery if you don't buy a ticket" thing. Staying on your customers and circling back and back again puts you in luck's path. Then, when and if it comes, you're there. Since you can't rely on its coming at all you might as well skillfully work your selling strategy and make a good living the old-fashioned way. You never know when your customer's muckety-muck boss might get a wild hair and decide that the entire worldwide organization needs your product—a lot of your product. Cha-ching. Would you consciously allow a few disappointments and setbacks take you out of luck's path? We didn't think so. But you probably do more than you know.

PESKY PERSISTENCE

Salespeople often confess to us that their lack of results is partly due to the fact that they aren't persistent enough. A lack of persistence is really just a lack of commitment. Think about how persistent you are toward things that you really want. How easily do you give up? When you will no longer tolerate not having what you really want in your life and in business, you will become more persistent in pursuing it. Desire will be in direct proportion with persistence. Do you think that kids need to attend seminars on how to be persistent? They were born persistent. Withering in the face of resistance is another one of those traits we tend to learn as we get older and will need to unlearn to get what we say we want.

A lack of persistence is a story you tell yourself that makes it okay to not have what you want. Instead of working on discovering what you are really committed to, you can just force yourself to become more persistent. That's not a terrific arrangement. If you aren't aware of the practical and emotional reasons why you want the things you want you won't be able to attach those powerful motivators to your persistent striving for success. The persistence you force upon yourself will be torture, and you'll find yourself procrastinating and unconsciously avoiding it at the slightest provocation. Heck, you'll avoid it without provocation.

To be effective over the long haul, persistence needs to be fueled by desire. Desire can be layered. Your desire to provide a secure and prosperous lifestyle for yourself and your family, regardless of what form that takes, is layered over your desire to feed the success of the company that provides you these opportunities. Those desires are layered over your desire to establish and maintain a compassionate relationship with your customers, truly helping them achieve the things they want. That's a large agenda. Roll up your sleeves and get to it. If the proper desires are layered on top of one another you'll have no problem sticking to it.

This is the point where you may become pleasantly annoying to your current or prospective customers. The way you transcend just plain, ordinary, garden-variety annoying, to pleasantly annoying, is with compassion.

Your customers must truly really understand that you care and that their best interests are paramount in your mind. Your persistence can actually send that message if you keep circling around and landing each time closer to their genuine concerns. You can't be phony. You must really care, and show it. Show it with the questions you ask. Your genuine curiosity about how your customers are feeling will make life easier. There is a difference between a hammer and a velvet hammer. If you belligerently continue to ask for their business without a strategy to move the conversation forward you have crossed the line and will soon wear out your welcome. You've also more than likely blown a shot at a return appointment.

Belligerence will reveal itself if you are not listening and asking enlightened questions. "What's your problem with this?" is not an enlightened question to ask a customer. "Do I have to spell this out for you again?" won't win any prizes either. "What part of this is beyond your comprehension?" is a favorite of the snotty-nose crowd. Compassion doesn't sound like, "Now I am go-ing to go o-ver this a-gain ver-y sl-ow-ly. Watch my li-ps." Customers can see through phony-baloney smiles as well. The only way to sell persistence on the basis of sincerity is to be sincere.

STALLING

If your current or prospective customer has not made a decision by now he or she may be stalling. For some reason he or she is putting off making a decision. We on the selling side of the equation are not the only ones vulnerable to doubt and indecision. Procrastinating, stalling, or otherwise putting off making a decision are basic human dynamics that you must learn to anticipate and deal with in your customers. If not, you may be giving up too soon and too often, and literally walking away from significant amounts of business. People are often reluctant to act, even when they've made their decision and action is in their best interest. Decision-delaying tactics are natural, and are another one of those anticipated obstacles that can nevertheless throw you off course. Think of it this way: It's your current or prospective customers' job to put off making a decision. Your job is to provide enough benefits and solutions so they can't resist acting now.

Why They Stall

It's fair to say that if you can understand some of the reasons that your customers procrastinate it will help you facilitate a solution that will overcome their concerns. Some of the reasons people can't or won't make a decision include:

- Fear that there may be a better deal somewhere else: Every retailer or other commercial enterprise that offers a double-your-money-back-guarantee-should-you-find-a-better-price-somewhere-else is attempting to take the better-deal-elsewhere mentality out of the equation. As long as customers can fantasize that they'll get the same thing you're selling (or better) from someone else or someplace else a lot cheaper, they will put you off. This is rarely the case (finding something better for less), but it can happen. The fact that it can happen is enough to keep them from pulling the trigger on your deal. Do you have a way to convince them that there will be no buyer's remorse about you or your product? Can you introduce your prospective customers to happy existing customers?
- Keep looking: When someone says they intend to keep looking they are probably thinking the same thoughts as above. Their imaginations are at work. Or they could be thinking that what you've presented to them is unacceptable, and they don't want to come right out and say it in so many words. "When you find what you're looking for," you inquire, genuinely curious, "what will it look like?" You then engage your customer in describing, in his or her own words, the product and deal you're offering. In short, you use your superior facilitation skills to gain agreement.
- Bad buying experiences: Many prospective customers fear that they are making a mistake based on disappointments they've experienced in the past. In other words, they don't want to be fooled twice, or for the third time. That's embarrassing and

humiliating, especially if they work for a sadist who relishes the opportunity to embarrass and humiliate subordinates as much as possible. This is a trust-building mission for you. Not only do you need to be completely authentic: You need to be persistent. The persistence we talked about earlier, and genuine compassion for helping your customers solve their problems, will forge the type of relationship you can build a career on.

- They're still confused: Overzealousness can bite you. In your exuberance you may have overloaded your current or prospective customers with too much information. Assuming they are on the clueless side, too much information can cause a meltdown. Customers don't ordinarily buy while in the midst of a meltdown. Information promotes thinking unless there is too much, too fast. Then information blocks thinking. You want thinking to give way to action as fast as possible. So be careful to provide food for thought. Not so much as to make them gag—just enough to keep the juices flowing in your favor.

- They may just be a suspect and not a prospect: Suspects can talk a good game and tie you up indefinitely, with no intention or authority to buy. What do you know about this person? Have you gone through any kind of qualifying protocol? How do you know this person is authorized to buy? Do you merely suspect you are talking to a person who can become a customer with the stroke of a pen? If so, you must be independently wealthy and have lots of discretionary time on your hands. Do your homework up front and make sure that you have a bona fide prospect on your hands, not just a suspect.

- Certain personality styles can't be rushed into making decisions: Detail-oriented, pragmatic, concrete thinkers need time to organize the information given before making a decision. The more you observe and study how your current and prospective customers process information the better equipped you'll be to feed them just the right amount at just the right pace. In *Unleashing Leadership: Aligning What People Do Best with What Organizations Need Most* (Hoover, J., & Valenti, A., 2005) the authors describe four primary leadership styles that you will be selling to at one time or another:

- ° Control specialists are hard-driving, bottom-line types, impatient for results. If anything, a control specialist will be impatiently tapping his or her foot, waiting for you to finish your canned 2-minute drill so he or she can buy what you're selling or throw you out.
- ° Compliance specialists are the high-itemization, everything must reconcile, follow standard accounting procedures ad nauseum, make you want to tear your hair out customers, who will detail you to death. If you present what you're selling in such a way that it appears to add up, you win.
- ° The social specialist is an emotive social butterfly who wants to know that whatever you're selling is going to promote peace on earth and goodwill to all. He or she won't give a rip if it makes money or punches up production. The social specialist just wants everybody to get along.
- ° The stability specialist wants to see that what you're selling will enhance efficiency and effectiveness. The stability specialist seeks to create a stable organization or a stable home through balance, shared responsibilities, and an equitable distribution of workload. Can you help?
- You've found a way to offend them: Sometimes people are land mines. We'd rather be a bull in a china shop than a bull in a minefield. If you're paying attention you'll pick up quickly on the idiosyncrasies that reveal the wild and crazy personality types that populate the planet. If you don't pay attention and plow through your presentation oblivious to individual leadership styles or personality characteristics, sooner or later you'll offend somebody. It will probably be sooner rather than later, and you'll be looking for another prospective customer sooner, too.

Handling a Staller

Here are four steps that can help you get hesitant current or prospective customers off the fence. Hesitant buyers often don't know why they are unable or unwilling to move forward and sign on the dotted line. Neither do they have a significant motivation to find out. But you do. As long as your customers are immobilized by indecision, you're twisting in the wind. This is where you take off your detective hat and put on the mortarboard and start teaching.

Step One: Identifying the Objection

Once again, "I need to think it over," or "I'm not ready to make a decision right now," could just be the smokescreen that sends your competitors or lesser sales professionals running for the parking lot. No matter what they say or do, you plan to stay put and take another shot at getting your customer's real concern out in the open. If you don't, you're just spinning your wheels and wasting everyone's time. You might as well head out the door with the weak-kneed crowd. As a sales professional, this is where your open-ended questioning skills are extremely important. These are the questions that move the conversation forward versus shutting it down. You need to step up in a nonthreatening way, and gather more information. Reestablish what your customer's true needs are, at the same time discovering what the real stumbling blocks are.

Step Two: Isolate and Address the Objection

Once the real objection has been identified you have another chance to confront the genuine concern and eliminate another obstacle, all the while moving the sale forward. One obstacle that may finally be revealed is the need for third-party approval. If your customer says, "I'd really like my partner (or whomever) to look this over," then you'll know better what you're dealing with. You can then say, "If you can acquire your partner's blessing, are you ready to move ahead?" If he or she says "Yes," then actively work to set up an appointment with the partner to get his or her approval. If he or she says "No," you can be assured the real issue has not yet been uncovered. It may be that he or she doesn't need anyone's approval, but might say so to buy time. Indecision reigns.

Step Three: Stimulate Urgency

Some prospects are just not willing to recognize the costs involved by failing to act promptly. This is your opportunity to explain what your current or prospective customer or his or her company may be giving up by postponing a decision. What are the values and benefits, emotionally and perhaps economically, for making the decision now instead of waiting? Plan for this appeal to urgency ahead of time and try and make the reason for acting now compelling. A well-argued case for urgency will make a customer feel remorse for not buying.

Step Four: Ask Again

Once you've isolated the real objections, addressed the concern, communicated urgency to act based on value and benefits, the only thing left between you and a closed sale is the signature on a piece of paper. It's time for your prospect to step up to the plate and take a swing at a decision. Some people need one more little nudge to put them over the top. Don't be hesitant to close the deal and ask for the order, especially when you know that it's right for the customer. If you really understand your customer's needs and desires, and you are looking out for their best interests, then they'll be glad you gave them a little push.

"I know it's a big step," you say, to empathize with his or her hesitation. Or use reverse psychology and minimize the commitment. Say, "This is a small step that will make a huge difference," or something to that effect. Ask them if the solution you provided makes sense to them. If it has, mission accomplished. If it hasn't, you may have taken your eye off the ball again, if just for an instant. Your future in sales is tied to your ability to ask and keep asking. Focus and stay focused. You will get what you ask for far more often than you'll get what you deserve.

If your current or prospective customer is still not willing to make a decision, go for the next best thing: start pushing for an appointment to meet and go over all of this again. If he or she is mere moments away from a decision you'll hear the decision before he or she will want to cover all that ground again. The willingness to meet again, even if the decision remains on ice, indicates a sincere interest in your product on the part of your customer. It could sound like this: "Mr. James, I appreciate the attention you're giving my product. I also understand how important it is for you to give this decision more time and thought. I know that once you've made your decision you'll stand by it completely, because of the tremendous value and benefit it will bring to your organization. When can we get back together to review your decision?"

Get a specific date and time. If he or she won't give you a specific time to reconvene, there is a message—and it should be clear to you what it is. Tell him or her that you'll keep calling until an appointment is set. Of course, you can button the whole thing up right now if he or she wants to sign off. Hint, hint. Signing off now might suddenly become more appealing than a threatened continued onslaught by you. You are passionately committed to helping your customer out. That must be clear. It's hard to turn someone away who is passionately committed to helping you.

IT'S IN THE CARDS

You also have to know when to hold them and when to fold them. Current and prospective customers who can't make up their minds can cost more than they are worth and can become a time-management issue. Sometimes there just isn't a match to be made. If you can honestly say that your product is not a good solution for your prospective customer, if you have made an honest and tireless effort, using every selling skill available to you—all to no avail—move on, and remember sales is and always will be a formula. The X-factor is you, and the independent variable is your customer. Sometimes they just won't give up their independence.

Raise your game at every stage: prospecting, appointments, presentations, contracts. Work on your skills to improve at every stage. The sales profession is not for beginners—it's for finishers. It doesn't matter where you start, what matters most is where you finish. Winston Churchill's biographers at www.winstonchurchill.org, a service of the Churchill Center in Washington, DC, claim that stories of his turbulent school days are more myth than fact. True or not, he preached the gospel of perseverance to the point of annoying his adversaries. Although we don't see customers as adversaries, if anything will ultimately pay off, it will be persistence.

On October 29, 1941, Churchill addressed the boys at his alma mater, Harrow School. "Never give in," he told them. "Never, never, never, never, in nothing great or small, large or petty, never give in except to convictions of honour and good sense. Never yield to force; never yield to the apparently overwhelming might of the enemy." Eloquent words that contain powerful advice to anyone interested in getting what they truly want from life. Passion, fortitude, enthusiasm, and resolve are the tools of all master salespeople, who can also look disappointment square in the eye and carry on in spite of it. Be a bulldog.

You already know that Michael Jordan was cut from his high school basketball team. But he circled back to play at the University of North Carolina and for the Chicago Bulls. In one of his most famous Nike television commercials, aired during the 2004 NBA playoffs, he explained: "I've missed more than 9000 shots in my career. I've lost almost 300 games. Twenty-six times I've been trusted to take the game-winning shot and missed. I've failed over and over and over again in my life. And that is why I succeed."

What does success look like Michael Jordan style? Olympic Gold Medal winning basketball team in 1984. NBA rookie of the year in 1985. Six NBA championship teams. Sheesh, the list is huge. Michael Jordan, like Winston Churchill, finished well what he set out to do because he persevered and will remain a legend long after he has joined that big all-star team in the sky.

MORE LESSONS FROM "NEVER, NEVER, NEVER"-LAND

We've talked in previous chapters about the tireless tenacity of children in asking for what they want, and how creatively they manufacture solutions, real and imagined, to sell us on the value of their getting what they want. To drive the point home we've decided to twist the lens a little on the kids thing. Despite the relentless pursuit of what they want, despite the often aggravating, percussive drumbeat of "I want, I want, I want," despite the fact that kids never, never, never, give up, there comes a day when they do. No matter how much they've worn us out up to that point. The day they give up and begin down that road toward adulthood complacency, melancholy, and cynicism is a sad day. Something in their lives is lost, never to be fully regained—if it's regained at all. If there is any lesson from the kids here, it should be to recover and restore as much as you can of that relentless tenacity and eternal optimism.

PERSONALITY-BASED ANNOYANCE

The risks of aggravating various extreme personalities vary. Proceed at your own risk. When you press the sale with different people they will push back differently. Different things annoy different people. When you turn up the heat with a variety of personality types be prepared for a variety of reactions. The finesse required to handle extreme personalities is one of the reasons you earn the big bucks.

Annoying the Machiavellian

If you push the envelope with a Machiavellian you might find out what a body bag looks like—from the inside. He or she won't mean anything personal by your murder. Please don't take it personally. Your mistake was to come off as a threat. Machiavellians see people in two ways: as threats or as assets. So rewind and regroup. When you want to come back at the Machiavellian one more time, turn up the heat, and get the order, pretend you're Tom Cruise in the film *Jerry McGuire* and plead to the Machiavellian to let you help him (or her). Plead to be on the Machiavellian's team and he or she might relent and give you and your product a shot.

Annoying the Sadist

If you annoy a sadist he or she might add righteous indignation to an already intense desire to see you squirming in pain. The decision facing you is whether or not the pain is worth it. Depending on what you have to gain from the sale, whether it be emotional gain, material gain, or both, it might be worth the suffering. But isn't that true of anything in life that's truly valuable? We tolerate discomfort, and sacrifice to have it. The sadist is just helping you pay your dues and is determining how badly you really want to succeed. If you show you're willing to take some of what the sadist dishes out, you might become one of his or her favorites.

Annoying the Masochist

The masochist will love it. Go ahead and get tough. Remember the customers who were chased away and came back begging to buy? Make sure you know the difference between a masochist and a Machiavellian. But that shouldn't be hard, even to a neophyte. The masochist will feel that he or she deserves to be mistreated for being so wishy-washy about making a decision. At this point you'll probably agree. As strange as it might sound, the annoyance step we're covering in this chapter can be just the type of aggravation some people are looking for.

Annoying the Paranoid

Annoy a paranoid personality and he or she will probably not react. It's more likely that paranoid personalities will interpret your intensified pressure as further evidence that the world is out to get them. What might catch them by surprise is the fact that the world *is* growing impatient to get them. You might succeed in arguing that you need the paranoid person's business badly, which explains the increased pressure. On the other hand, the paranoid personality might be beyond trust, and anything you say will push him or her further away. Unlike the masochistic personality, aggravation might not be what the paranoid personality is looking for.

Annoying the Greek God or Goddess

If you're not careful here, it's thunderbolt city. Similar to the approach you made to rattle the Machiavellian's cage, you might want to throw yourself on the mercy of the small-*g* gods. Imagine you're sitting before Donald Trump, sweating bullets, about to be fired. That's the small-*g* god thing at work. If you annoy him by crossing him you're likely to get canned. End of story. Beg to sit at the foot of his throne and do penance for your sins and transgressions and he might begin to dig your style. You might get the order because the small-*g* gods ultimately lack the infinite patience of the Big-*G*. Go ahead and wear them out.

Annoying Your Best Buddy

It's probably impossible to annoy your new best friends. The harder you try the more they might like it, if only because you're paying them so much attention. As we mentioned before, you'll need to attach an ultimatum to your last approach at overly needy customers. If there is a chance to make a game out of your one-approach-after-another-approach approach, they will play along. Leaving is what will annoy the emotionally needy customer. That's your ace in the hole.

Annoying the Decent Soul

Decent souls are well-balanced and well-grounded in reality. They know you're a professional. They know you have a job to do. They won't be taken off guard when you persist right out of your comfort zone. They will either calmly explain that they intend to keep the boundary right where it is and you can save the act for *American Idol*, or they will nod and say, "You really are serious. I didn't realize this meant so much to you." There's an opening you can drive a truck through.

CHAPTER EIGHT SUMMARY

Oftentimes your current or prospective customers will test your sincerity by holding out longer than you might expect. On the other hand, they might not want what you're selling, or they might not want to buy it from you. It happens. One way to test the theory is to circle back and ask for the order again—long after any normal person would have folded his or her tent and gone home. But you're extraordinary. Your resolve is greater than your current or prospective customer's resistance. Or not. You won't know until you try. Pilots call it pushing the envelope. Nuclear scientists call it tickling the dragon's tail. For you, it's going to the edge of your comfort zone—and then some.

- Teach your customer how to buy: By giving up and going home, you only teach your customers how not to buy. If the message is, "The more you resist, the deeper I'll excavate to find your genuine concern and address it," your current or prospective customers will learn to come clean sooner and save themselves the inevitable aggravation and annoyance of making you come and get it, because you will.
- Failure is your friend: Because it chases away the weak at heart, leaving the spoils to you. We prefer "disappointment" to the word "failure," but you get the point. The more you experience disappointment the more you're motivated to learn methods and techniques to avoid it. The more often you experience disappointment, the more assured you are that you're operating at the edge of your competence.

- Passionate persistence: If you are persistent to the point of becoming slightly annoying, because you're going through the motions recommended by some book called *How to Sell to an Idiot,* you're being the idiot again. Stop it. You're persistent to the point of becoming slightly annoying because you're so passionate about the act of compassion you're engaged in that you can't help yourself. Now doesn't that sound better? It sounds better because it is better.

- Customers stall because: They're afraid they'll find a better deal the moment after they sign on your dotted line and they'll look like idiots to their idiot bosses. They might have also had some bad buying experiences. Perhaps they're still confused. Whatever the reason, there's nothing here that you can't fix with your skilled questioning and problem-solving techniques. Each time they resist buying, circle around again, each time a little smarter.

- Use empathy: Psychology is like your car's transmission. It works in forward or in reverse. There is no sideways. If your customer hesitates to buy because it's such a big step you can empathize and say, "I know this is a big step, but I'm here to make sure you get through it with flying colors." Or slam it in reverse and say, "This is really a small step when you compare it to the value and benefits you're going to enjoy. Spending so little to gain so much. You'll be the hero." How thick you pour it on is up to you. However, you must first decide whether your current or prospective customer's transmission is in forward or reverse.

We've pushed you as far out of your comfort zone as we're going to. You're about to enter the warm and fuzzy world of appreciation. We won't coach you to feign false appreciation. In the next chapter we'll coach you to count your blessings. Your current and potential customers are both on that list—even if they are a little clueless. They're on that list even if they're a lot clueless.

9

STEP NINE: APPRECIATE

You've worked your magic. You've done your job by helping your current or prospective customer solve problems, earn more money, appear younger, taller, and thinner, and/or generally live a happier life. Now thank your customer and leave. Two things here: Thank your customer appropriately. Don't start to cry, fall to your knees, start kissing rings, or otherwise embarrass yourself, no matter how badly you needed the sale. Fall to your knees, burst out in tears, and thank God in the parking garage. It's better to have security spot you and call 911 than to fall apart in front of the customer you just spent 30 minutes convincing you are brilliant. Second, don't act like you now have the rest of the day off and try to spend it with your new friend. Make like Elvis and leave the building before he or she discovers how annoying you can really be off the clock.

Good salespeople not only know when their time is up—they also know how to make a graceful exit. Whether you've landed the big sale or not, be grateful for the opportunity your current or prospective customer has given you. At the conclusion of your presentation be sure to thank those who were present at the meeting. Then thank anyone else on your way out who was instrumental in your getting the appointment. You may need them again somewhere down the road.

The receptionist may be your number one ally, and you may be the only source of acknowledgment and appreciation he or she enjoys. Many managers simply don't show appreciation to those who make their lives easier on a daily basis. They tend to take them for granted. You have a lot to be gained by taking on the role of appreciation monitor and giver. Not only is it the polite and right thing to do, appreciating people like the receptionist will pay dividends. It's enlightened self-interest. He or she knows everything about the company and is likely the most underappreciated person in the organization. The receptionist is an ongoing wealth of knowledge, can put your call through or put you on hold, and knows when your current or prospective customer is in a good mood or breathing fire. If you've made the receptionist part of your team, he or she can help open the door of opportunity for you.

Gratitude is easier to bestow on others when things are going well. When you've made a sale you're in a more benevolent and sharing mood than when things are falling apart and you're walking out with your tail between your legs. Nevertheless, gratitude is a state of mind. It's one of the habits of successful people because it's never solely dependent on results. Acknowledgment, appreciation, and gratitude play big roles in the success of the most successful salespeople.

THE SELLING CYCLE

Every sale has a lifespan. There is a beginning, middle, and an end. There is an opportunity to build and keep the momentum going during each stage. Showing appreciation throughout each of the stages is also important. Appreciation positions your mind properly so as not to transform pushback and rejection into an abscess of resentment. Once that happens—and your mind might be headed in that direction long before you realize it—you're in trouble. Your current and prospective customers will sense your reservoir of resentment long before they've done anything to contribute to it. So will everyone else in your life. Resentment has an odor that's hard to mask. It's best to not let it take root to begin with.

The Beginning—Prospecting

In the beginning you are engaged in prospecting and setting appointments. You are spending a tremendous amount of your time, energy, and effort just for the opportunity to meet with your current or prospective customers. During this stage there are people helping you meet your objective every day. Don't wait until after you've landed the appointment to thank those who got you in to the dance. Don't just feel appreciative—act appreciative.

Concentrate on showing appreciation throughout the day, especially during the beginning stages of a sales cycle. We've talked about connecting with your current and prospective customer. But don't forget to make a connection with everyone else who plays a role in your success. Actively look for people to acknowledge. Make it a game. Send a minimum of five appreciation notes every day. You'll need to buy them by the case, not in packages of eight.

You can gain a lot of mileage by sending a handwritten, personal note to every one of those lovely receptionists you come in contact with day-in and day-out. This may seem a little rigorous for the average salesperson, but not so for top producers like you. Top producers know the benefits of having an insider on their team. An acknowledgment of appreciation at this stage can be priceless.

A short note to the receptionist could sound something like this: "Thanks, Mary, for your professional courtesy and pleasant telephone voice. I look forward to meeting you in person when I'm in your office visiting Mr. Jones at 11:00 on Tuesday the 8th. Thanks again." The appreciation monitor has struck again. Mary may have no idea who you are when she receives your note, but the next time you call or stop by the office where she works, you'll be remembered the moment she hears your name. That thank-you note could still be on her desk 2 to 3 weeks later. You may have also provided a helpful reminder of that appointment on her boss's busy calendar.

You will be in her favor from then on. A simple thank-you note can reduce the challenge of getting in front of the people you truly need to see. It's like shooting layups on a 9-foot rim instead of the regulation 10. You almost can't miss. The price is also right. The possible return far outweighs your investment in a postage stamp, thank-you card, and envelope.

The Middle—The Appointment

Once you arrive at your initial appointment and announce yourself you will be welcomed in a more positive way if you appreciatively presaged your arrival. Be sure to announce yourself in such a way that the receptionist puts two and two together. "Hello Mary, I'm So-and-So. Here's my business card." It's identical to the one you included in your note. "I have an appointment with Mr. Jones at 11:00," you continue. You want to help Mary connect every dot possible so you'll hear, "You're the one that sent me that nice card."

If your thank-you card isn't still on her desk, remind her that it was you that sent it: "Did you get my card?" Then thank her again in person for being so pleasant on the phone when you called. When you see Mr. Jones be sure to brag on Mary. Tell him what a delightful assistant he has and how professionally she has treated you. Mr. Jones likes to hear good things about people he works with. Should your compliment get back to Mary it will be icing on the cake. Invoke the same type of third-party compliment with Mr. Jones by telling Mary how nicely he treated you. She might not believe her boss is a particularly nice guy, but positive vibes beat negative vibes any day.

The Ending—The Presentation

There are many possible outcomes from presentations to your current or prospective customers. The first and foremost is making a sale. Remember: Expect to win. There could also be other, less favorable results from your sales appointment. Be prepared for a variety of responses. Whatever the response, you need the feedback to plan your next move. Appreciate it. Be grateful for it. Everything your customers do in response to you is valuable knowledge.

It's interesting that most salespeople are okay with feedback as long as it's positive. We love to hear how fabulous we look and how enlightening our presentations are. Who wouldn't want to be asked if we've lost weight or been working out? We have no problem receiving that kind of feedback. Positive feedback has an immediate effect on how we feel about ourselves, a direct hit on our self-esteem.

When the feedback turns sour, in your opinion negative, it has the exact same effect. Your self-esteem takes a hit, but in the opposite way. You will be told, "No." "Don't ever call again." "You look worn out." "Are you all right?" "Your product s****" (is inferior). When you hear that kind of feedback, don't forget, it's still just feedback. You can ruin your entire day by taking what others say personally. Feedback is the compass that can lead you to the next step in your strategy to get what you want. Use it accordingly. Don't let others have the power to take the wind out of your sails or rain on your parade.

MAKE IT MEMORABLE

So whatever the outcome of your presentation, favorable or seemingly not, don't let it adversely affect the form or sincerity of your appreciation for the opportunity. Appreciating and being grateful for the opportunity is a decision you can make without anybody's help. Likewise, nobody can make you unappreciative or ungrateful without your permission. In every stage of the sales process focus on making your acknowledgment and appreciation memorable.

Always send a handwritten, hand-addressed, and stamped (not metered) thank-you card to the current or prospective customer like you did to his or her receptionist. When someone receives a telephone message or personal note, it is much more powerful than an e-mail. Your customer may receive 100 to 200 e-mails a day. The chances of your e-mailed appreciation/thank-you note getting read are slim and none. Even if he or she sees it, it won't be as special as something written by your hand or spoken with your voice.

How many personal, handwritten notes do you suppose he or she receives a day? Five? Three? Probably one. Yours. Be appropriate in your acknowledgment, but be memorable. You can always use humor in your thank-you notes, the way you do to break the ice and ease everybody's nerves in presentations. It can be fun picking out a cache of humorous cards at the stationery, drug, or grocery store to send to your customers. Most importantly, don't take your current or prospective customers for granted. If you don't tell your customers thank you, someone else might, and it will probably be your competitor.

THE BATTLE FOR MIND SHARE

All salespeople author their own reputation. They forge their own style. Having a reputation as someone who is an overacknowledger isn't all bad. It beats being labeled and thought of as ungrateful. It's an area of selling where we suggest you err on the side of too much versus too little. You capture your customers' mind share before you capture their market share.

Creating a system for acknowledgment and appreciation into your overall sales strategy is as important as planning and prospecting. The only difference is that with planning and prospecting you are generally able to see a direct return on investment. Acknowledging and appreciating others won't always be so visible in the effect it has on your business. You must be willing to show appreciation unconditionally.

What do your customers say about you when you're not around? What do you want them to say about you? Do the two match? If they don't, go to work to make sure they do. Your reputation is really the only thing you have complete control over. You may not be able to predict the exact level of success that you will experience, but with reasonable certainty you will be able to mold yourself and your reputation into the salesperson you want to be.

It is extremely important to do everything in your power to forge a strong and positive bond between yourself and your current and prospective customers. When your competitor is calling on your customers you're not there to defend yourself, your product, or your company. The image and reputation you've forged must sustain you in your customers' minds—in your absence and while you're under assault.

Not everyone you send a note to is going to call and tell you what a thoughtful person you are. The fact is that few if any will call and acknowledge your gesture. Some will toss the card and never give it or you another thought. It's just the cost of doing business and holding up your end of the bargain; to keep the momentum and commitment going in thanking and appreciating your customers for the opportunities they provide. If you are emotionally invested in receiving recognition from those you show appreciation to and acknowledge, you're doing it for the wrong reasons.

In sales you win by inches, not miles. The little things add up. When you consistently do the little things right big things go right. Everything counts. Termites do more damage than earthquakes. Every day you are trying to produce a slight edge for yourself. That's all you need. In basketball or football they call it a step. You don't need a mile. All you need is a step on your opponent and you can score the basket or the touchdown. The difference between the top salespeople in the world and those that are at the bottom is often very slim. Focusing on small stuff such as gestures of appreciation and gratitude can put you over the top.

THE PRESENT

We urge you to immediately get in touch with your gratitude gene, because you truly have something to be grateful for. Send a gesture of appreciation right away. Don't put it on your to-do list for later. Candy, golf balls, flowers, whatever is appropriate to the size and scope of the opportunity or payoff. You were a detective in your customer's office. What did you observe that he or she liked? Is he or she a tennis player? Hockey fan? Antique car buff? Quilter?

There are plenty of clues as to what would make an appropriate "thanks for the business" gift if you pay attention. Sending a gift, like sending a handwritten card, shows your customers that you're thinking about them when you're not in their presence. You didn't just bolt out the door mumbling, ". . . sucker." If you know what's good for you don't forget to include your customer's clerical assistant in your generosity. It's not one or the other. It's both.

MORE LESSONS FROM CHILDREN

Kids know the power of bearing gifts. The crude bouquet of wildflowers a little boy or girl picks for Mommy. The apple for the teacher. Cooking breakfast for Daddy and then waking him up at 6:00 AM Saturday morning to serve it in bed. The endless artwork they draw, paint, cut out, and paste. It's not so much the fact that children bear gifts to express their gratitude to us as parents and relatives. We see them do it generation after generation, without prompting. They come by giving tokens of esteem naturally.

The lesson we should learn from their generosity of affection is the impact it has on us. Who isn't completely won over at the presentation of the bouquet of wildflowers, the apple, Daddy's breakfast in bed, or the endless artwork they draw, paint, cut out, and paste? Granted, the relationships are more distant and civil, but personal tokens of appreciation and gratitude from you to your customers and the people that help you see your customers demonstrate how much you value them—just like kids bearing gifts is an expression of how much they value us.

PERSONALITY-BASED APPRECIATION

Different personalities appreciate different things. That doesn't mean you should avoid demonstrations of your appreciation. But it's important to show the type of appreciation that will most resonate with the personality type you're dealing with. Like everything else you learn through observation and interaction with your current and prospective clients, the things that make them unique are the things that create unique opportunities for you to connect with them in meaningful ways.

Appreciating the Machiavellian

Knowing how obsessed the Machiavellian is with reaching the top of the corporate and/or social ladder, you can immediately score appreciation points by pointing out how much you appreciate the fact that he or she is in a position of power and influence. The only way you could appreciate him or her any more than you already do is if he or she were in a position of even greater power and influence. This doesn't mean you're fake or disingenuous. If you have customers who are Machiavellian by nature and you have a good shot at selling them in the future, you want their future to include a successful climb toward more power and influence. More enlightened self-interest.

Appreciating the Sadist

This is a toughie. The types of things that sadists do rarely evoke appreciation. But you're a professional. If it takes reaching down a little deeper into your bag of tricks, you can do it. You can invoke your superior empathic skills and touch the sadist where he or she is rarely, if ever, touched. "I appreciate the fact that you're in a position with the power to make this kind of decision," you say honestly, remembering that power is important to sadists. "And I appreciate how much you suffer to maintain this status." Because you're aware that sadists are simply sharing the pain they already feel inside, your reference to their suffering will fall on receptive ears.

Appreciating the Masochist

Masochists suffer, too. The difference is that they feel they deserve it. Instead of using energy to pass on the pain to others, as sadists do, masochists work on creating circumstances that will cause them to experience more discomfort. All you need to do is slightly tweak your references to suffering. The masochist believes that he or she suffers. You should state your appreciation that they're willing to suffer for the greater good of the organization, family, community, you name it. Others are happier for the suffering the masochists do, which makes masochists suffer all the more by comparison. As with the sadist, the masochist will feel understood and appreciated if his or her suffering is acknowledged and positioned properly.

Appreciating the Paranoid

As with every other extreme personality type, the paranoid person paves the way for you to show appreciation. Just read his or her signals and follow. Since paranoid people feel the rest of the population is conspiring against them, they feel as if they're carrying a heavy load. "I'm glad that you have the strength and ability to hold up under the kind of pressure you're faced with day-in and day-out," you empathize. "I appreciate the fact you're willing to do business with me in the face of everything else you must deal with." There's no reason to be more specific. The paranoid personality will fill in the blanks. But he or she will appreciate that you took the time to express your appreciation for his or her desperate situation.

Appreciating the Greek God or Goddess

These folks practically demand to be appreciated. Therefore, practically everything you do around them is designed to show your appreciation and gratitude. Since they believe they are more or less omnipotent to begin with, everything that takes place happens because of their divine providence. What's not to be grateful for? If they see you, be appreciative. If they buy from you, be truly appreciative. Small-*g* gods and goddesses don't require you to perform acts of penance. Well, not often, anyway. Mostly when they're really bored; regular acts of penance require too much bookkeeping on their part. Acts of appreciation on your part, sincere and genuine as they may be, will be interpreted by the Greek gods and goddesses you deal with as acceptance of your role as dutiful subject in their small-*k* kingdom.

Appreciating Your Best Buddy

This is sort of like pouring gasoline on a fire. But it's also a good opportunity for you to get in touch with how much your new best friend is helping you. It's easy to feel as if you're the one doing all the helping when someone seems to be sponging off you emotionally. You might hesitate to show appreciation to an emotionally needy person because it will encourage him or her to clutch tighter. We suggest you think of it as positive reinforcement. It's behavior modification. Show appreciation when your new best friend buys, therefore encouraging him or her to buy more if he or she wants to experience more appreciation and gratitude from you. Of course, your token of appreciation can be something as simple as time with you at lunch or on the golf course. Even so, you want the order and/or account to be big enough to justify the sacrifice you're making.

Appreciating the Decent Soul

Decent souls will probably beat you to the punch. They will actually appreciate you for bringing your wares to their doorstep. Decent souls can keep things in perspective because they're so emotionally mature. They're not going to think you're doing them an enormous, self-sacrificial favor. They know you're getting paid for what you do. So keep it real. When you send notes or appropriate tokens of your appreciation attach a sentiment that is a genuine expression of how their willingness to see you, hear you out, and buy from you brings opportunity and possible extra value to you. It's not that decent souls have omniscient powers to know what you're thinking (the way the small-*g* gods believe they do). Decent souls appreciate your honesty because they know in a commonsense way that you're human and not that much different from them or anyone else.

CHAPTER NINE SUMMARY

Appreciation helps you, the sales professional, maintain perspective. It's possible to gain so much success that we begin to think that it's our wonderfulness that makes it all happen. It's not. It's our current and prospective customers' willingness to see, hear, and understand the truth in our story. Without that, our wonderfulness won't fatten up our kids or get us that new bass boat we've been wanting. In the same way, resenting customers for not buying won't help your future prospects, either. Appreciation is a good habit to develop. Appreciate, appreciate, and appreciate some more.

- Appreciate your way to the top: In Chapters Seven and Eight we wrote about failing your way to the top, and how failure is your friend. You don't need to make such a stretch to realize how appreciation is an extremely valuable tool in your skill set. Being appreciative and demonstrating appreciation are not extracurricular activities. To be truly successful you need to become darn good at it.
- Appreciate throughout the sales cycle: Appreciation and gratitude are not just appropriate at the end of the cycle. There are excellent opportunities to be appreciative and grateful at the very beginning of the cycle, when people agree to see you, right through closing and moving on to new business. The more ways you can discover to maintain your appreciative and grateful attitude in every aspect of your personal and professional lives, the better positioned you will be to make friends and influence people.
- Make it personal: Sending someone a canned message via e-mail is like a form letter in snail mail. It won't gain you much. A thank-you phone call is your voice, live and in real time—even if you leave a voice mail message. Your current or prospective customer knows that you took the time and effort to make the contact. A handwritten note also shows that you took the time, away from your time with your customer, to think of them and demonstrate your appreciation. Personal touches are the most professional.
- Make it memorable: Include some humor and/or a snippet of information that's unique to your customer or the relationship

you have with your customer. By making the message unique and personal you will sear it into your customer's memory. Think about the gestures you've received that stuck in your mind. The positive ones. How can you make tokens of your gratitude and appreciation stick? Whatever they are, you'll get the most traction from acts of appreciation when they're all about the customer.

- The battle for mind share: Besides being the best way to keep your thinking right vis-à-vis your current and prospective customers, showing appreciation is yet another way to connect and stay connected with the people who pump lifeblood into your veins. This is even more important when you consider who else is showing his or her appreciation to your customer: your competition. You want that prestigious front spot in your customer's mind, but so does your competition. It's not just a battle for your customer's mind, it's a war—and the stakes are high.

- Use your own experience as a guide: You know how empty it would feel if children suddenly stopped showing appreciation and affection in their innocent and often crude ways. You don't want to cause your customers to feel that same sort of emptiness. They know they're making your life better when they buy from you. If you show no appreciation they will begin to feel used. That won't make them want to see or buy from you again. Get to know each customer's personality type; when you demonstrate your gratitude and appreciation, do it in a way that they will appreciate the most.

Now that you've added appreciation to your growing arsenal of superior selling skills it's time to layer the acts of appreciation and gratitude with the knowledge that you're in business to grow your income. For that you need referrals for new business. That's where we go next—in search of your next customer.

10

STEP TEN:
GET A REFERRAL

Idiots know other idiots. Geniuses know other geniuses. Idiots don't know many geniuses. Geniuses know a lot of idiots. But they don't suffer them kindly, as a rule. However, the idiot's inner idiot knows the genius's inner idiot, although the genius denies it. The genius denies it, that is, until it comes time to give a reference to a salesperson.

Sometimes idiots are the only people who will talk to each other at parties. If you find yourself only talking to idiots at parties, well, you do the math. The more you resonate with your customers, the better, regardless of at what level. Again, it's about asking. You don't need to say something idiotic like, "Do you know anybody else dumb enough to buy something from me?" Nor *would* you ask such a thing—given your undying belief in yourself, product, and company.

You're a lot better off asking where he or she plays golf (if you see a putter in the corner). "Oh, yeah. Doesn't so-and-so belong to that club? How's his business these days? He might see the wisdom in something like this, too." Ask what schools the kids attend. Those serpentine conversations can unearth lots of new prospects.

Selling to people your customer is familiar with is a way to protect yourself against cancellations. If your customers refer you to someone they know, both current and new customers are less likely to bail on you. Of course the opposite is also true. If your customers are dissatisfied with what they received from you, either in product or service, they may never order again or offer a referral. Worse yet, they'll probably tell others of their experience. Their stories will likely be exaggerated, more horrific, and larger than life. If you really hack off your customers and they angrily pull the plug they're likely to wage a telephone campaign to everyone they know and warn them about you, your product, and your company. Even an idiot can use the telephone. E-mail might be tough, but they're all over the phone. Deliver what you promise and stay on your toes if you want to avoid death by speed-dialer.

FEAR NOT

Referrals are the lifeblood of every successful salesperson and business enterprise. Yet, like orders, most salespeople are terrified to ask for them. One reason could be that your customer had a poor experience with your company and you're afraid you'll get your head pinched off. If that's the case, getting a referral is the least of your problems. In most cases it's simply that "afraid to ask" thing again.

Generating referrals starts with you, the salesperson, truly believing in your company, its products, and/or services. Earlier we said that you have three sales to make to every current or prospective customer: You, your product, and your company. You can believe in yourself all you want, but referrals and ongoing repeat orders will be directly linked to your customers' overall experience with your product and in dealing with your company.

Asking for referrals is important to growing your business. But it shouldn't come at the expense of your current customers. We look at both repeat business and referrals as positive. However, it's commonly accepted among salespeople that it costs seven to eight times as much in money, time, and other resources to locate and secure a new customer as it does to keep your existing customers happy. Referrals diminish the locating costs and the effort required to earn a new customer's trust. "One-Order Wonders" often cost more than the company gains on their sales. This is one way that companies sell themselves out of business. Ask for referrals, but use discretion and a sense of balance. If your customers have enjoyed you, your product, and your company, you're asking them to share the love.

BUILD CHAMPIONS

It's not enough to simply build a stable of satisfied customers. One of your goals should be to get more champions on your team. You don't always get referrals automatically, despite doing a good job at satisfying your customers. Your customers expect to be satisfied. Having satisfied customers tells you that they were pleased with you, your service, and/or your company. Beyond that, you must try to create customer champions for you, your product, and your company . . . all three.

If you've garnered some champion customers they will let you know that you exceeded their expectations, and they will tell others on their own, in addition to offering up referrals. Earning a champion customer is like adding another salesperson to your sales force. The bar had been raised. Today you must knock your customers' socks off. Your level of service must be beyond reasonable, predictable, and consistent if you expect to receive referrals and repeat business.

One of the best ways to exceed your customers' expectations is to start by asking them what those expectations are. Salespeople often brag about how they're going to exceed someone's expectations without bothering to ask about expectations. Once you've discovered what's important to your customers, as in their hot buttons, zoom in. Now you have clear targets and defined expectations to exceed. More importantly, you know where your customers' benchmarks are so you know where exceeding their expectations begins. You'll never know that without asking, "What does a successful purchase look like afterward?"

GET SOME HELP

Future referrals are dependent on your entire company stepping up and exceeding customer expectations. It's more than the merchandise showing up on time. Post-closing referrals come from the overall experience, and it has to be positive, top to bottom, inside/out, and beginning to end. The salesperson can do a great job taking the order, but if customer service, delivery, and accounting drop the ball, say good-bye to your referrals.

Post-closing referrals have everything to do with your customers' overall experience working with you, your product, and your company. It's about total accountability. Everyone in the company has to be focused and committed to gaining referrals and repeat business. It can't just be the sales department. Teamwork is a lot easier to talk about than to deliver. Everyone is committed to the idea until someone or something messes up. All of a sudden the team shrinks and you begin to hear, "It isn't my job."

Not only does the concept of teamwork fade, so do the referrals and repeat business. It is evident when real teamwork is in action versus just being the slogan of the month. Our definition of simple is simple in concept, but much more difficult to live. "Teamwork is the absence of blaming, complaining, and gossip." How does the company you work for measure up, using our definition of teamwork?

How can you become the champion within your company for those who contribute to teamwork and customer satisfaction? Share your customers' delight at the performance they receive from your company. Publish positive (and critical) testimonials in your company newsletter. Make special recognition of those who stand out in customer service. These people are making you money. Extend your appreciation and gratitude far beyond your customers to include everyone who contributes to your success. Do everything within your power to make sure an attitude of gratitude and appreciation permeates your organizational culture.

GET THEM TALKING

You'll be able to tell if you've knocked your customers' socks off. They'll talk to you about the experience. More than that, they'll describe their experience to others. When you suspect that your customers are talking you up, thank them. Then ask them who they've been talking to. You don't need to ask permission to use your current customers' names. If they have been bragging on you, your product, or company, the new contacts already know who you are. As a courtesy, ask your current clients if they mind you contacting the person or persons they've spoken to.

Tell your current customer that you want to extend the same type of help to their friends, associates, and colleagues. Often they'll offer to make an introductory call for you. Everybody likes to pass on good news. The impulse to pass on good news is almost as strong as the uncontrollable urge to sound the bad-news warning when they've had a bad experience. Knock their socks off and you'll get good referrals. Cheat them out of their socks and you'll get talked out of business. In this way you establish a foundation for productive and mutually beneficial relationships that can pass the test of time.

By doing your job happily, confidently, and enthusiastically, you have every reason to expect referrals that are given happily, confidently, and enthusiastically. People want to tell other people when they have experienced something that they consider extraordinary. Think of the last time you went to a new restaurant and it was outstanding. You couldn't wait to tell your friends. It had to be outstanding at every stage to get your endorsement. They couldn't just be good at taking your order or only good at bringing the bill and taking your money. Just like every sale has a beginning, middle, and an end, so did your dining experience. They had to hit the mark on all three to get your referral—and so do you.

GET AN "A" FOR ASKING

The best way to ensure you receive referrals is to ask for them. Remember: you don't get what you deserve. You get what you ask for. Just because people want to refer someone to you doesn't mean it's their job to remember to bring it up. It's your job to bring it up.

Asking for referrals is another form of prospecting. By now you should have figured out that we believe everything you do is somehow connected to prospecting. Older sales models suggested that you find prospects, qualify them, make a sale, and then ask for a referral. With this old approach you grow your database one transaction at a time—at best—and if your customers cancel their orders, you might lose the chance to add them to your database at all. Getting a referral up front is a form of insurance. In case the customer cancels, you at least have the referral he or she gave you.

We hear salespeople say all the time: "I just need to get more referral business." That's usually not all they need to improve their professional performance. But it is important. Generating more re-ferrals requires being more proactive. You don't get sales—you make sales. Getting more referrals isn't going to happen by accident, either. Success is not a coincidence. Neither is generating a pool of referrals.

Generating a pool of referrals requires a well-thought-out strat-egy that you incorporate into your daily activities. It will have no more importance than you give it. Asking for a referral must be a part of your prepared presentation, no less important than asking for the order. If it isn't included in your presentation, more times than not it will get left out. Then you'll probably blow it off. "I forgot to ask for a referral before ending my presentation," you'll think afterward. "No big deal." It is a big deal. It's a lost opportunity.

Asking for referrals is another one of the success habits used by top sales producers. It is not something they remember to do some-times. It is something they ask at the end of every sales presentation and conversation they have. Top salespeople tell everyone they meet and everyone they know what they do and who they work for. They can get a business card out of their wallet faster than a speeding bullet. Asking for referrals is why they network. To top producers, it's not about net-eating, net-smoking, net-dating, or net-standing around. They understand that networking has the word "work" in it. It also has the word "net" in it. You're working to cast your net to haul in a big catch. They also know that you can't put a price on a third-party endorsement.

There are many ways to ask, some more subtle than others. After enjoying a meal at your favorite restaurant, leave one of your busi-ness cards with the tip. On the back of your card write, "Thanks for the great service, I hope I can return it to you someday." The back of your business card is always a great place to write a thank-you note.

Ask How It Went

Send a survey to your customer at the completion of your transaction to see how you did. You can call it a customer satisfaction survey, meant to ensure that your customer is satisfied. But you really want to know how you did and where you can improve. First of all, wouldn't you like to know if you really knocked their socks off? If so, what was it about your presentation and follow-through that did the trick?

By asking your customer to grade your service you create another opportunity to ask for a referral. Send a small enticement and thank-you for their time in completing and returning your "report card." Tickets to the movies, restaurant gift certificates, or Starbucks certificates are some suggestions to give as a thank-you. It's the thought that counts. The returned report cards also make good testimonials that can be used for new clients.

Ask with Appreciation

Be sure to also show your appreciation to those who refer business to you. If tokens and gestures of appreciation and gratitude are appropriate for those who merely agree to see you, think of how valuable it is for someone to help you see others with a warm referral to open the door. Always follow up to let your referring customer know how the appointment went with the person they referred. This also gives you the chance to ask for another referral.

Let the referred person know how you got his or her name. This is a way to deliver a third-person compliment. Report to the new prospect that the referring party said good things and thought that meeting you would be beneficial. They'll quickly get past some of the anxiety that comes with new relationships. There is comfort in knowing that if you did a good job for someone they know, you'll probably do a great job for them as well.

The likelihood that your customers will give you referrals is directly tied to their satisfaction with you, your product, and your company. The best way for you to be assured of receiving ongoing referrals is to take care of your customers, tell the truth, and over-deliver. Self-generating referral business starts with providing your customers exactly what you said you would provide, and more.

MORE LESSONS FROM CHILDREN

We've talked about the natural skills that kids possess as they relate to selling. Asking for referrals is no exception. Companies and salespeople spend millions of dollars every year to learn the skills they've had all along and merely forgot. You've seen kids in action developing referrals. They know that their best insurance against a "No" is asking for a referral, especially if the person they are pitching may not give them what they want, when they want it. That's why kids typically increase their odds by getting a referral. Asking for a referral can be a thinly-veiled threat.

"What's Grandma's telephone number?" "Can I write to Grandma on the computer?" Just the threat of taking their request to another party is sometimes enough to make us capitulate, knowing that the kid is going to escalate. Kids teach us every day that the best route to getting what you want is the direct approach. They put us on the hook, and the only way to achieve any peace in our lives (get off the hook) is to cave in.

Make it easy for someone to give you a referral; put them on the hook. Don't say, "Bob, do you know anyone I can contact that may have a need for my product?" That makes it too simple for Bob to just say "No." Asking a closed-ended question like that almost invites a "No." Ask instead, "Bob, who do you know that may want to take advantage of the same offer I've given you?" Instead of asking, "Do you know . . . ?" ask "Who do you know?" Kids are good at wording questions in such a way that "No" is not an answer.

PERSONALITY-BASED REFERRALS

You need to ask yourself what will inspire the different personality types you're dealing with to spread the gospel of you, your product, and your company. People give referrals as a gesture of gratitude for what you've done. They also give referrals as a way of generating new business for themselves. They might give a referral because they want a vendor or supplier to do a better job for them. There can be all kinds of reasons. Being the detective that you are, your job is to find out what's in it for them.

Referrals from Machiavellians

Is giving you a referral going to help a Machiavellian reach the top of the pyramid faster? If he or she thinks so, you'll have your referral. Better yet, you'll have as many referrals as you can handle. Your challenge will be to make the Machiavellian believe that giving you referrals will help his or her career aspirations. You can dwell on how others will appreciate the way you, your product, and company can make their lives easier and how you'll make sure they remember that it was the Machiavellian that made the referral. Machiavellians like having people owe them. They like to have as many aces in the hole as possible when it's time to bust their move to the top.

Referrals from Sadists

We don't recommend that you make the experience of working with you, your product, or your company so painful that the sadist wants to share the experience far and wide. Sadists do like having power and influence to impose their nefarious agendas on weaker and less powerful victims. That's your play. Like the Machiavellian, you want to make a big deal of how referring you will give the sadist more power and influence. Of course, what he or she does with it is his or her business. You're not responsible for that. There's no vice in giving yourself every good advantage to weave the wonderful magic you weave, no matter what your referring party's motives are.

Referrals from Masochists

Masochists feel as if they are bearing the weight of the world on their shoulders. They also feel as if they deserve to bear the weight of the world on their shoulders. But they feel it all the same. You therefore have the opportunity to feed the masochist's sense of self-denial by making life easier for others. Masochists will immediately recognize the gut-wrenching value of making life easier for others. That, once again, is your angle. You don't want to be so insensitive as to suggest that masochists feel diminished by the success and happiness of others. Masochists will fill in those blanks themselves. You can stick to your mission to provide the best solutions available to your current and prospective customers' problems. Have no fear of asking your masochistic customers for referrals. If your continued success will make the masochist more miserable, you'll get them.

Referrals from Paranoids

Paranoids are not so eager to help others. Why should they? Others are out to get them. This makes referral generation more difficult. Your best angle is to position your request for referrals as a window into the operational motivation of others. "When someone gives me an introduction to a prospective customer who could benefit and find value as you have," you tell your paranoid customers, "I report back on how that relationship is going and to what degree my new customers are benefiting from the same types of solutions you're enjoying." To the normal person that makes you an open line of communication and goodwill. To your paranoid customers that makes you a mole. Why not? You're no more responsible for what paranoids do with good information than you're responsible for how sadists and Machiavellians use the power and influence you help them attain.

Referrals from Greek Gods or Goddesses

Small-*g* gods and goddesses are not punitive, fire-and-brimstone types, unless you really tick them off. They actually enjoy being benevolent to mere mortals. Granting you referrals is a way that you can become their evangelist. If not an evangelist, you can at least be an instrument of their goodwill to the population of the planet. Once Greek gods or goddesses become believers in the solutions you bring to their problems, they won't hesitate to spread the message— as long as they feel it's their message. That's how you position it with them. This is a solution they had the wisdom and judgment to employ. Don't put yourself in the position of being the wise one, or they might think that you're trying to climb up on their throne. Give them the small-*g* glory and they'll give you the referrals you seek.

Referrals from Your Best Buddy

Make it sound like a party and you're in. Offer to keep your new best friend better connected to others he or she might have had contact with in recent years and your new best friend will become an open address book. The paranoid personality wants to know what's happening in other people's lives as an early warning system for counter-espionage. Your best buddy customer simply wants to have more friends.

Make it sound as if you're expanding his or her social network, which, in a way, you are. Helping others win friends and influence people is a great way for you to do the same. Thanks, Dale Carnegie. You're actually providing a great service to people by keeping their networks alive and well. Your best buddy customers will appreciate it more than anybody.

Referrals from Decent Souls

Decent souls understand what you're in it for. They want a better life for themselves and their families as well. Like your best buddy customers, decent souls appreciate the value of a healthy social and professional network—although not in such a needy way. You need to earn the respect of your decent soul customers, so that they will feel you're worthy of becoming a member of their network. They take personal and professional relationships seriously.

If you perform for them the way that you're capable of performing, with all of the professionalism and enthusiasm you're capable of, your decent soul customers just might grant you entrée into their networks. This is a high honor. Once you're granted access to a decent soul's network the other decent souls you'll find there will consider you in high regard, based on who is recommending you. Congratulations.

CHAPTER TEN SUMMARY

Like anything else you badly want, it's better to come right out and ask than to hope your current or prospective customers will read your mind. Be completely honest about your desire to gain referrals, so that you can share the solutions you've already offered your customers with others they know who might benefit as well. If you have been the stand-up sales professional we hope you've been you will have earned a place of trust and respect in your customers' hearts. That's your ticket to the dance.

- Referrals are not manipulation: You believe in your honesty and professionalism, the quality and reliability of your product, and the reputation of your company. You don't need to mumble when you ask for the names of others with whom you can share this good news. Show your pride. You're not looking for suckers, you're looking for other people as intelligent and insightful as your current customers.
- Earn your referrals: You shouldn't expect to be given referrals out of the goodness of someone's heart. Some people might try and earn a living on the kindness of strangers, but those will be the ones with skinny kids and old cars. Demonstrate that you

deserve referrals by the way you conduct yourself and by the way your product and company perform for your customers.

- Juice the conversation: Even when you have proven your loyalty and unassailable work ethic, it might not occur to your customer to provide you with the names and contact information for others who can use what you're selling. You need to engage them in a conversation about people they come into contact with at the golf course, the bowling alley, or anywhere they encounter folks—but don't necessarily connect the dots.

- Referrals are yours for the asking: Above all, learn to ask. Like the concept of closing early and closing often, you need to ask for orders and referrals as part of your premeditated, rehearsed, methodical, systematic approach to selling. AEAO is as good a motto as CECO. Don't reduce your status as a sales professional to that of the also-rans by forgetting, or worse, avoiding the question.

- Pump up their network and yours: You can be a great facilitator of contacts for your customers. Share your referrals with them. Even if your customers are not in direct sales, you nevertheless encounter all kinds of people they could benefit from knowing. If you are an expert manager of social and professional networks, thereby keeping relationships and introductions alive and well that your customers might be neglecting, they will no doubt appreciate it. At the end of the day, they'll feel more comfortable sharing referral information with you because of the congenial and professional way you handle it.

All of the wonderful methods and techniques you use so skillfully work in concert with one another. Although sequence is important, especially in developing new relationships, there comes a time when your customer relationships are cyclical, like the seasons of the year. Following up with your customers could be thought of as something you do at the end of the process. But it's actually a new beginning, as you're about to see.

11

STEP ELEVEN: FOLLOW-UP

The last thing you want is to think, "Now that I have the order my work here is finished." Your work here is just beginning, Bucko. Following up is one of the best ways to stay off your laurels and on your game. Other than prospecting, follow-up is one of the weakest links in salesmanship. We agree that once you have an order in your hot little hands there is tremendous relief. That's natural. But once an account goes on autopilot it's easy to sit back and bask in the renewals. Lean back too far and you'll fall on your bask. Autopilot is not selling. Once you stop selling, your income will begin to dwindle—slowly at first, then faster and faster—until you can't remember what you were so happy about when you closed that big sale.

Follow-up is selling, every bit as much as prospecting and asking for orders and referrals. Follow-up is a good way to snag orders that were just out of your reach the first, second, or third time around. That's new business, Bucko. If your inner idiot has a solid simpatico going with your idiot customers, why not sell them more? You could say that following up is cleaning up after yourself. There might be lots of crumbs left following your big feast. Those crumbs add up. If you ignore them or sweep them away you might be costing yourself and those who depend on you a lot.

Most people prefer the home run to a base on balls. Why not? It's more dramatic. Why bend over and pick up a dime when you can wait to find a dollar? Because it all adds up, that's why. A buddy of ours likes to emphasize the value of small successes by saying, "My eleven dimes will beat your dollar any day."

NO COMPETITION

There is a fine line between being a pest and being persistent. Being persistent is being professional. Following up means staying in touch. That might be troubling to some customers who thought they were finally rid of you. In those cases, you need to demonstrate the value of what you're doing. In other words, keep selling. Following up is caretaking. Asking for appointments to check and make sure your customers are getting full value and benefit from what you just sold them is a courtesy. Call them courtesy appointments.

It's a shame that follow-up is such a weakness for so many sales-people (right behind prospecting, asking for orders, referrals, etc.), because showing courtesy can eliminate about 40 percent of your competition. After your customer has made the decision to buy from you, you have the inside track. Imagine you're driving an Indy 500 Formula One race car against all of your competitors in their race cars. Reselling or up-selling your current customers is like passing your competition on the inside of a curve. We've already mentioned that you can eliminate about 50 percent of your competition by working smarter, harder, and more creatively through the prospecting, pitching, asking for orders, and referrals stages. Skilled follow-up can eliminate another 40 percent.

Altogether, you can effectively block around 90 percent of your competition where your primary customers are concerned. The last 10 percent can be a real dogfight. But as you narrow your field of competition it becomes easier to focus all of your energies on winning the key battles. This kind of 90 percent dominance, with a solid customer base, is definitely doable. That's why we say you really have no competition if you put your mind to it. Okay, very little competition. If you could clone yourself you would likely bankrupt your competition. The only chance they have is because there's only one of you.

WE HAVE SEEN THE COMPETITION AND IT IS US

The biggest competition you have is your inner idiot telling you to back off because enough is enough. This lack of motivation is the fiercest competitor you'll face on any given day. Misplaced priorities represent more competition. Too many salespeople spend too much time focusing on whether they appear knowledgable and trustworthy to their customers, and become too timid to stay engaged, lest their customers see through them. Knowledge and trustworthiness are important qualities, but not to the exclusion of follow-up and follow-through. Consistent follow-up and follow-through are the best ways to earn your current and prospective customers' trust.

Salespeople complain all the time that they never hear back from their customers. The truth is that they're leaving the continued contact with their customers to chance. It's not your customer's job to follow up with you. That kind of wishful thinking is another competitor—much more deadly than a salesperson for a competing product and company. Unskilled salespeople don't have any form of structured follow-up program in play. That's why their telephone's not ringing and their mailboxes are full of cobwebs. Sales managers and independent salespeople spend too much time and money on management and skill-building programs without a system for the most critical part of the picture: following up and staying in touch.

PUT FOLLOW UP INTO YOUR MIX

Following up is where the top salespeople earn extra effort points. At the end of the day, extra effort points are redeemable for cash. Faithful, friendly, and consistent follow-up is your shoehorn to lasting relationships and more business. You must be fanatical about follow-up, using every medium available to you: telephone, e-mail, facsimile, handwritten notes, smoke signals, carrier pigeons, as well as your smiling face, up close and personal. Learn enough about your prospects to know the best medium and methods to stay in contact and turn them into customers. It takes no special talents and abilities to follow up, just a conscious awareness of how valuable it is to do. To follow up or not to follow up is a critical choice you face every day.

Hungry and motivated salespeople intentionally and deliberately include follow-up in their daily prospecting routines. Following up after a sales call or an actual sale reflects urgency in a salesperson. Urgency is a quality that will add to your income. You can't afford to wait for your customer to call you back and beg to do business with you. They have more urgent things to do with their time. At least their agenda is more urgent in their minds. They may be right or they may be wrong, but their minds are where the game is played.

Following up after a sales call or an actual sale shows that you care about not only making the sale, but that you also care that your current or prospective customers are given all the information required to make and continue to make decisions in your favor. Following up will also help reveal the actual commitment on the part of the prospect. If more time or information is required you'll know it, and you'll be able to deliver it.

Many prospects evaluate the kind of service they will receive from you based on how quickly and consistently you follow up. Losing a sale due to a lack of follow-up on your part is not only regrettable, but a dagger in the heart of your future earning potential. Follow-up is another of those basketball-ian metaphorical layups that you just can't miss. Unless, of course, you blow it.

TIME HAS NOTHING TO DO WITH IT

Too often we hear salespeople lament that there's not enough time to follow up. That makes about as much sense as trying to pass your competition on the outside of a curve when the inside is wide open. Time—or lack of it—is one of those stories that underachievers use to justify performing below expectation and potential. When salespeople are not producing there must be a reason—a story, if you will—that lets them off the hook, in their own minds, anyway. Major story themes include the weather: too cold, too hot, too rainy, or too windy. Have you ever heard, "People just don't buy in weather like this?"

The economy is another scapegoat for underachievers. "I haven't been able to sell a thing since (fill-in-the-blank) moved into the White House." How about holidays? Have you been told that people won't purchase anything around Groundhog's Day, Easter, or Christmas? Many salespeople believe that the stories they conjure up provide some sort of safety net for nonproduction. Don't even get us started on astrology and planetary alignment.

Not following up is a choice and a decision—not an affliction. Those who don't follow up sales calls and successful closings are still good people. They simply have a flaw in their sales system. At least one flaw, anyway. Top producers always have time to follow up. Following up doesn't slip through the cracks in their daily sales routines. They don't follow up some of the time. They follow up all of the time. The top producers' follow-up schedules look something like this: Prospect.

PRE-SALE, PRE-DELIVERY, POST-DELIVERY FOLLOW-UP

Follow up to schedule appointments. Schedule appointments. Pre-sale follow-up. Present the product or service. Follow up to teach more about your product or service. Close the sale. Pre-delivery follow-up. ("Just want to give you a head's up that your order shipped today. Is there anything else I can do to help?") Deliver the product. Post-delivery satisfaction follow-up.

Any idiot can see (we did) that follow-up is the second piece in every step of the sales process. It needs to be an automatic step in every stage of your overall sales strategy. Follow-up creates additional selling opportunities, the chance to express your appreciation and gratitude, an opening to ask for referrals, and a chance to learn more about what someone might need from you.

Following up leads is critical to your overall prospecting success. If you commit to a daily contact goal but never plan for follow-up, your success ratio will drop dramatically, or never take off to begin with. Make sure you have a follow-up system ready as part of your business plan. Whether it's mailing out thank-you notes, sending additional information, a telephone call, an e-mail, or a personal visit, just do it.

IT'S RESEARCH

Never take repeat business for granted. Some salespeople are so elated to make the sale they simply forget to make after-the-sale follow-up contacts. The after-purchase follow-up is critical for a number of reasons. First, it's an opportunity to let your customers know how much you appreciate their business. In addition to finding out their level of satisfaction you'll be able to keep tabs on how well your company is backing you up with fulfillment and delivery. Were your promises delivered on time by your support team? Without this follow-up call, how will you know where you can and need to improve?

Most of the time if your customers are not happy with any part of your product or service they won't take the time to tell you. They'll just quickly disappear and never be heard from again. The moniker "One Order Wonder" applies to customers as well as to salespeople. Failure to follow up can cost you more than just one customer's future business. They're likely to go on that all-out counterendorsement campaign we warned you about.

WHEN?

The word *when* is another secret weapon of top salespeople. Sometimes you have to come right out and ask your customers when you can follow up, especially those who need to think things over. Ask them when you can check back. When can you meet again? Most people don't like the word *when*. It evokes commitment and accountability, two things that most people try to avoid at all costs. But without using the word *when*, how will you know when to follow up?

Without a *when* the conversation will simply dangle in midair. How many of those dangling conversations do you have going on right now? You know the ones: "I'll call you, we'll have lunch, I need to give your proposal more thought," and so on. The next time someone says to you, "Let's have lunch sometime," take out your day planner on the spot and, with pen or pencil poised, ask them, "When?" Then watch his or her lip quiver. "Oh my goodness, she (or he) really wants to go to lunch," the customer thinks. "I always thought the word 'lunch' was a metaphor for 'until we meet again.'" Most of the time your customer will offer lunch at some undisclosed place, time, and date just to get rid of you. Let your customer know you won't be dispatched that easily. Use the word *when* and be prepared for your customer to be confused. They're not used to making commitments, especially when someone intends to follow up.

Commit to follow up in three distinct areas every day:

- New business: All of those new prospects you are developing on a daily basis.
- Old business: Past clients. Follow up and check in to see what's changed since you last contacted them.
- Current business: Those customers that you are currently working with.

It's simple. You need to get up, dress up, show up, step up, and follow up every day. Oh, and remember to Churchill them—never give up.

MORE LESSONS FROM CHILDREN

This is where kids fall down on the job. They really don't follow up on past transactions. They immediately begin new ones. They'll follow up indefinitely until they get the answer they want. Kids have no compunction about asking again and again until they get the answer they want. They also don't have a problem, once they get what they want, in asking for more.

Have you ever noticed how kids follow up? "Is it five minutes yet?" "Is it five minutes yet?" "Is it five minutes yet?" Talk about pleasantly annoying. Maybe they develop a technique called "annoying your way to success." Either way, it's just another lesson from the world's greatest salespeople.

Kids also learned at a very young age how to use that four-letter word that drives most adults crazy—"when?" Tell kids that you will take them to the park later and their first word is "when?" They know that all adults have a "when" button and they know how to push it. We bring this on ourselves when we say, "I'll tell you when it's time." They keep asking "when?" until you commit to a specific, unambiguous time. Then they hold you to your promise. It's amazing how a 7-year-old 50-pound child can make a fully-grown adult feel surrounded and helpless just by using the word "when?"

PERSONALITY-BASED FOLLOW-UP

You need to be ever mindful that different folks intuit information differently. They flash on various stimuli in a variety of ways. This is as true of follow-up as anything else. As you follow up with customers who represent different personality types it's important to do it in the style, tone, and medium that make each individual customer feel the most comfortable and supported. This is hard for many salespeople, because sales techniques and sales behaviors are often taught in a one-size-fits-all mentality. If everybody had the same personality, the same likes and dislikes, the same comfort zones, selling would be so easy anybody could do it. But they don't. People don't respond equally to the same follow-up approach and not everybody can sell. You can sell to your heart's content, because you recognize these differences and can use them to your advantage.

Following Up with Machiavellians

Let Machiavellians know you're solidly behind them. They're only going to see you in one of two ways no matter what. You're either an asset in their ascent to the top or you're an impediment. Your follow-ups should be check-ins on how their plans are proceeding and if they are receiving the recognition they deserve. By checking to see if they're receiving recognition, you're acknowledging that they deserve recognition. Remember, you're asking permission to help them.

To Machiavellians, recognition is an indication that they're about to be moved up the corporate food chain. If they don't receive the recognition they feel they deserve they're going to hack their way up anyway. So you might as well help them feel comfortable with their ambitions. If Machiavellians truly believe that you're helping them climb their ladder, your follow-ups will be welcomed, and their loyalty to you will be directly proportionate to the loyalty they believe you have to them.

Following Up with Sadists

Use follow-ups to keep pushing the point home. The product and service you're providing to the sadist will help him or her maintain or even increase the power to do their dastardly deeds. You wouldn't say it in so many words, of course. But you get the point. By conducting predelivery follow-ups to remind sadists of the wonderful thing they have done by buying from you, they might get so giddy in anticipation that they up the order. It's about power with sadists, and follow-ups at every stage of the sales process give you a chance to reinforce that. Sadists won't necessarily feel compelled to bully you, especially if you use your continuous follow-up opportunities to re-assure them that they're in control.

Following Up with Masochists

Reminders are good if you're reminding them how badly they'll feel when everyone else is feeling good. Masochists can wear you out with their eternal self-pity. Sometimes you just want to slap them. On the other hand, you can't control how other human beings feel. The fact that a masochist feels badly when doing what's best for everyone else only coincidentally coincides with the fact that you want your product and the service you deliver to make people's personal and professional lives better. If it works all the way around in some sort of quirky manner, that's all the better. Follow-ups are continuing opportunities for you to reinforce whatever message needs to be delivered to each personality in a way that suits his or her agenda. Just tell the masochist how well your product is working out for everyone.

Following Up with Paranoids

Paranoids are super interested in staying informed. Your paranoid customers will see your continuing follow-ups as a good, ongoing source of reconnaissance data on their enemies list. You, of course, are merely sharing news of your encounters with others inside and outside the paranoid's organization. If your paranoid customers want to use that information to stay one step ahead of the conspirators, that's between them and their conspirators. You can appreciate how the interaction that takes place as a result of constant follow-up is appealing to all of the various personality types. As long as you're scratching where each one of them itches, your follow-up will be appreciated.

Following Up with Greek Gods or Goddesses

Small-*g* gods can always use some good-natured reminding. Lest you begin to believe their press as much as they do, remember that small-*d* deity is not omnipotent. They only think they're omnipotent. Likewise, they are not omniscient. They only think they are. If they were truly all-knowing and all-seeing they would realize that they're not all-knowing or all-seeing. They're just self-aggrandized imitations of the big *G*. Feel free to follow up and remind them of all the magnificent things they are causing to happen by working with you and your company. Remember your place. Don't get carried away and brag about your accomplishments in the presence of people who think they are gods. As long as you keep your correspondences suitably humble and reverent, follow up to your heart's delight. May your follow-up help bring to you the things that delight your heart.

Following Up with Your Best Buddy

Make a game out of it. Make sure your follow-up is often, but irregular. Regular contact with your new best friends might spoil them. B. F. Skinner, pioneer of modern behavioral psychology, proved this sort of thing with rats. But it's not that big of a leap to see how the principle applies to certain customers. Regular follow-up is good for establishing new behaviors on the part of your best buddy, but intermittent reinforcement is how to make it persist.

If you don't want to take our word for it, ask William Crane: "Therefore, when we begin to teach a desired behavior it is best to begin with continuous reinforcement, but if you wish to make a desired behavior last it is best to switch to an intermittent schedule of reinforcement."[1] In other words, follow up with your new best friends and follow up often. Just don't let them set their watches by you.

Following Up with Decent Souls

Decent folks appreciate the follow-up. If they're satisfied and contented for the moment they'll tell you so, pleasantly but firmly. Don't dig deep into your bag of tricks to try and compensate for their eccentricity the way you sometimes must do with Machiavellians, sadists, masochists, paranoids, and the emotionally needy. Decent folks are short on eccentricities. Play it straight with decent souls. Playing it any other way will teach them that you can't be trusted. We like to begin with the assumption that everybody we deal with is a decent soul, until they begin to demonstrate otherwise and we need

[1]Crain, W. (2004). *Theories of development: Concepts and applications* (5th ed.). Upper Saddle River, NJ: Pearson.

to adjust accordingly. Follow up whenever possible with the decent souls you work with and try to deliver fresh information whenever you can.

CHAPTER ELEVEN SUMMARY

Like every other aspect of your selling skill set, follow-up has more benefits to you and to your customers than meets the eye. You can continue to learn more about your customers. Knowledge is power. You can continue to share the value and benefits of your product with them. You can capture missed opportunities to close more business. Intelligent, appropriate, and consistent follow-up will be seen by your current and prospective customers as follow-*through*. Wherever customer trust is important, which it always is, follow-through is a big thing.

- There is no beginning: There is no ending. If you want to be technical, there is a chronology to prospecting, making initial calls, and pitching. Unfortunately, many salespeople take the chronology too seriously and think that receiving an order is the end of a sales cycle. To us, a successful close marks the beginning of a beautiful friendship. Follow-up and follow-through keep that friendship alive and growing.
- Avoid laurels at all costs: When we think in terms of linear accomplishments, it's easy to convince yourself that a successful close proves you're the bomb. Go ahead and pat yourself on the back. But don't pause. The pat should propel your forward, faster than before. Being ahead of the game is not the time to slow down. A successful close simply means that you got it right that time, and that you need to engage as many customers as quickly as possible now that you know what you're doing.
- You really have no competition: Unless others are as alert, informed, skilled, and persistent as you are there is no reason why they should pose a problem to you. Working smarter, harder, and more creatively will move you ahead of about half of your competitors. Persistent and skillful follow-up and follow-through will allow you to slide ahead of another 40 percent. That leaves ten percent for you to battle with. We lied a little.

You still have competition; just a lot less than you initially imagined.

- Follow up at every stage: When you're prospecting, follow up until you get the appointment you're seeking. Then follow up to confirm it. Once you've met with your prospective customer, follow up to confirm what you learned about his or her needs. Follow up until you get the order. Once you get the order, make a pre-delivery follow-up to coordinate and make sure you didn't leave anything lying on the table. Once your product is delivered follow up to make sure everything is meeting your customer's satisfaction. Follow up your follow-ups as often as you can make positive contact and keep the sales cycle alive.

- You have the time: To claim that there isn't enough time to follow up is the same as saying you don't have the time to sell. Follow-up and follow-through are critical selling skills. How will you make sure you're capturing all of the information you need at every stage of the game if you don't maintain follow-up contact? How will you be able to demonstrate you're there for your customers over the long haul without consistent follow-through? Selling without follow-up and follow-through is pure luck.

As the children teach us, follow-up is nothing more than another sales cycle beginning. It's good for you and it's good for your current and prospective customers. These concepts are admittedly simple to grasp. But they're rarely carried out to the point of being effective. That's why we've tried to help you lighten up on yourself and your customers. When you can truly put your profession and all that it requires for success into proper perspective, you have a platform from which to operate more effectively, more efficiently, and more profitably. There's only one method for continuous improvement of your performance: practice.

12

STEP TWELVE: PRACTICE

Athletics make a good simile for professional selling. No matter what heights a world-class amateur or professional athlete attains, his or her life is filled with practice, practice, and more practice. He or she will spend exponentially more hours practicing than competing. The same is true of an opera singer or a virtuoso instrumentalist. Many more hours are spent in the rehearsal hall than on the concert stage. The only time a professional or world-class amateur athlete stops practicing is when he or she retires and is out of the game for good. Many opera stars and virtuoso instrumentalists continue to practice their craft long after they've become too old and frail to perform in public. Think about that. Like the man carrying the violin case on the streets of New York, the impulse to practice and dedication to their craft is such that the practicing continues long after their performing days are over. This isn't true for everyone, but it's true for the great ones.

Cluelessness can be overcome with practice. Idiots can't think themselves into enlightenment. But they can act enlightened. At that point an idiot customer and an idiot salesperson can walk shoulder to shoulder with the Einsteins of the world. For what good is enlightenment if it's not in action? Enlightened behavior might come naturally and easily to the genius, while the clueless creature might need to study and rehearse hard and long. In the end, enlightened behavior is enlightened behavior. Even the dimmest bulbs among us can shine if they practice long and hard enough.

We didn't leave practice to the end because we think you should wait until all is said and done before you practice. You should practice all of the time. Work is practice and practice is work. The learning and rehearsing should never stop. Like an athlete or a musician, with a continuous commitment to getting better at what you do, these skills and methods should become second nature to you. That's when you can expect your best results.

The couple in Chapter Five on their first trip to New York just wanted directions to Carnegie Hall. When the wife spotted a man walking down the street carrying a violin case she figured he must know the route they would need to follow. When he told them that the only way to get to Carnegie Hall was to "Practice, practice, practice," he answered her question from his own truth.

When you buy a book like this or attend a seminar to learn new selling skills or sharpen the skills you have, are you looking for a roadmap to follow? Are you seeking the secret path to fame and fortune? If so, here's the news, which isn't really news at all: The truth you must face is that you already know 90 percent of what you need to know to attain your desired fortune and fame. What you might still be holding out for is a way to get there easily, effortlessly, painlessly, with no rejection, no conflict, and no risks.

The world's greatest salespeople don't eliminate effort, pain, rejection, conflict, or risks. They minimize those things through practice. Like great athletes, they receive constant instruction, coaching, and spend countless hours rehearsing. Despite all of their natural ability, they still practice. That's simply what the great ones do. Selling to idiots might seem as simple as falling off a log. Yet some will sell more to idiots more often than anyone else. Those will be the practicers. Every call you make is an opportunity to try something new as well as polish something used before. Trial and error is great as long as the errors are not life-threatening.

DON'T SUCCEED AT BEING AVERAGE

In any game you attain skill and excellence by getting on the field of action and practicing. Whether it is sports, business, or in life, practice must become a frame of mind. Most people succeed only at becoming average. That's the very definition of average. But there's nothing keeping your performance average. Nor is there anything that will place your performance above or below average except your personal resolve—or lack of it.

It's by practicing and by maintaining a commitment to continuous improvement that you will reach the top of your game. The two hardest things to deal with in life seem to be failure and success. Both are choices. You have the ability to close the gap between where you are and where you want to be, with practice. There are no shortcuts or secret road maps. Our definition of enlightenment is an alignment between insight and action.

Insight is the keen knowledge of what it takes to do the things necessary to succeed. Action requires the willingness to put those principles into practice, day-in and day-out, regardless of your present mood or the way the world is treating you today. No matter how much average salespeople know intellectually, we won't label them enlightened until we see some action. The right actions don't care if the doers have IQs in the 200s or closer to our golf handicaps. It's the action that produces results.

BE IMPATIENT

Continuous improvement means an ongoing effort spurred on by a lack of contentment and tolerance for the status quo. The impatience of the most successful people in life is upward and constant. The pages of business history are filled with stories of leading companies that did not change or strive to improve continuously. The stories don't end happily. The same is true of individuals. You will need an even more positive attitude toward change and practice to reach the next level of personal production. Change, practice, and continuous improvement are not optional.

Make sure you are practicing on the field every day, in real time. Talk to more people. Actively seek out what you don't know. Practicing not only produces improved performance, practice uncovers opportunities where they were not evident before. Look for those areas where you could get a little bit better and then a little better still. For the best results you must get better in critical areas. Practicing and reviewing your performance strengths and weaknesses will reveal what more needs to be learned.

One of the biggest differences between top-producing salespeople and underachievers is how they use their time. We remind you again, don't squander it. Time is your number one asset. Stay focused on high priorities and improve incrementally on everything else. If you must procrastinate, put off daily activities of little value. Here is an example of what getting a little bit better can produce. An extra 30 minutes a day devoted to prospecting can truly produce incredible results. If you think half an hour won't amount to much, consider this: After taking out Christmas, 30 minutes a day adds up to 182 hours per year.

Since a 40-hour work week averages out to 173 working hours a month (163 if you allow for usual vacations and holidays) using an extra 30 minutes a day, every day, will give you more than a full month of added productive time each year. You will have 13 months a year versus your competitors' 12 months. This is surely enough to make a big difference in accomplishing your goals. So the question becomes, are you willing to use the power of 30 minutes, starting to-day? You can see the dramatic difference practicing anything an extra 30 minutes a day can produce.

PERFECT PRACTICE

Be sure with all your practice that you're improving. It's possible to think you're practicing when you're not. If you're not focused on what you're doing the practice won't sharpen your skills. Are you making reasonable progress toward your goals? Without progress, practice is meaningless. More specifically, lack of progress indicates that the practice is not taking. Practice does not make perfect, as we've all been told. Perfect practice makes perfect. If you are not making progress, stop practicing what isn't working and try something new.

What if practice is all there is? What if there is no destination, just practice? Legend has it that the Aikido student asked the Master, "How long did you practice before you became an Aikido Master?" The Aikido Master replied with a refined question. "Do you mean, 'how long before I realized there is only practice'?" If you want to wax philosophic, the "all is practice" philosophy can decrease the fear of rejection. If you are only practicing, how can anyone offend you? "Don't ever call me again!" shouts a disgruntled prospective customer. "No problem," you think to yourself. "I was just practicing, anyway."

Practice will create confidence. Practice also seems to increase your chances at getting lucky. Practice asking for what you want and you're more likely to get lucky. Practice following up and you're more likely to get lucky. Luck is a choice. You can choose to be lucky every day. More specifically, you can choose to put yourself in luck's path, like the locomotive we spoke of, should it decide to come along. Vince Lombardi said that luck is where preparation meets opportunity. Our definition of luck is where preparation and opportunity meet action. Practice is the action part. Luck and opportunities are not predictable except that they are bound to pass by sooner or later. Practice makes you ready when that happens. Practice might even hasten the opportunities.

DANGERS OF PERFECTION

You don't have to be perfect to win, but you must start to finish, whether you win the race or not. Perfection can be procrastination in disguise. It can cause delay of game. Practice in front of real customers. Don't get hung up on illusions of perfection. Practice leads toward perfection. Being perfect doesn't lead to more practice. Spend less time role-playing and more time prospecting. You will never make a sale role-playing or practicing in front of a mirror.

Be willing to experience disappointment and make adjustments. All meaningful success is preceded by small failures; fail yourself forward. Don't dehydrate your dreams by playing it safe. There is no such thing as losing as long as you're still in the game. It isn't about being the best. Doing your best counts most. Losing is just an opportunity to learn how to win. The greatest salespeople in the world started their careers at the bottom of the sales force. They made many mistakes that exposed their imperfections on their way up. If salespeople waited for things to be perfect before exerting effort, no effort would have been exerted, and the great salespersons would never have achieved greatness.

Keep in mind that sales success is ultimately measured in numbers. It always has been and always will be. Intention plus commitment plus practice equal desired results. Despite practice and persistence, there's no need to be unreasonably enmeshed with closing the sale long after it's time to move on. We agree with the commonly used sales mantra: "Some will. Some won't. So what? Next." Keep moving forward. In sales as in life, pain is inevitable, but suffering is optional. Do more of what works. Do less of what doesn't. Practice every day and make intelligent decisions about what you will incorporate into your daily routine.

CARING EQUALS CHANGE

Don't become complacent about change and about practicing your craft. All self-improvement comes from change and practice. Self-improvement books and positive thinking can set the stage, provide you with principles, introduce you to new information, and remind you of things you know but have forgotten. There are plenty of positive thinkers out there with skinny kids and cars that burn oil. How many of them do you know? The biggest difference between them and you is getting the same thoughts out of your head and into your hands, where they become action.

Most people who don't like change dig themselves some pretty deep ruts. They claim that the ruts just happened unconsciously over time because they never consciously thought about change. The truth is that the ruts deepen over time as they purposefully avoid thinking about change. There was intention in their omission. Change for some invokes fear of the unknown. For them the certainty of misery is better than the misery of uncertainty. They only practice what they are familiar with and then complain that their results aren't changing. We've all heard insanity defined as the expectation of different results while doing the same thing over and over again. True insanity is knowing that, believing it, and not altering our behavior because of it. That's nut soup.

Complacency breeds indifference, and the indifference to change and self-improvement is what will open the window of opportunity for your competitors. We belong to the camp that believes that to earn more, you must learn more. That continuous learning is your mental fitness program. If you don't intentionally, deliberately, and continuously pump up your mental health, you don't need to worry about any competitors beyond the one in your bathroom mirror. You are more than enough to stop you. Once you get past yourself as a roadblock, anybody else is a piece of cake to overcome.

FLAT TIRES NEED CHANGING

The areas of your business and life that need the most developmental attention are usually the hardest to address. If prospecting is weak, salespeople often decide to work on their closing to increase sales—even though that's not the flat tire. When we see this kind of misdirected self-improvement we immediately ask, "What is the strongest part of the selling skill set?"

The no-brainer answer we receive is, "closing."

"Why are you changing the tire that isn't flat?" we press.

"We enjoy changing that one," they reply. "It's more fun than changing that prospecting one.

"Do you like to play golf?" we continue.

"Love it," they say enthusiastically.

"Which part of your game costs you the most unnecessary strokes?"

"Putting," they blurt out, without so much as a moment's hesitation. "Missing those two and three-footers really adds up."

"How much time do you spend each week practicing your game?" we ask.

"One to two hours every Saturday morning," they say proudly.

"Where do you spend those one to two hours?" We're getting suspicious.

"At the driving range."

"What are you doing at the driving range?"

"Hitting drives with Big Bertha."

"Didn't you just say that you needed to work on your putting?" we ask incredulously.

"Sure."

"Then why is Big Bertha out of the bag instead of your putter?"

"It's more fun to hit drivers than to practice putting," we're told. "Putting is boring."

Don't look for golf scores to go down any time soon with this kind of thinking. Likewise, don't look for your annual income to go up as long as you spend your time on the most pleasurable elements of your sales cycle and not the ones that need the most help. Don't change the fully inflated tire on your car just because it's easier to jack that corner up versus the one that's ground level.

WHAT ARE FRIENDS FOR?

Clinging to old habits will suppress your personal and professional growth. Clinging to old friends will do the same. We have nothing against friendship. But when you begin to change and grow as a person and as a sales professional your old buddies are going to start perspiring in an air-conditioned office. "What are you doing?" they'll ask nervously.

"Just practicing the areas of my sales cycle where I have the most trouble finding traction," you answer, with all the confidence of someone who is actually getting something done—as opposed to just doing something. "What are you doing?" you inquire.

"Polishing our pitches," they say.

"How many appointments do you have?"

"None so far. But when we do," they assure you, "we'll be ready. Do you want to go to lunch with us and talk about what we'll do when we get appointments?"

"Sorry," you reply. "I have a lunch appointment with a prospective customer."

They all exchange nervous glances and shift their chairs a few inches further away from you. One brave colleague walks over, rests his hand on your shoulder, looks you straight in the eye, and says, "We're worried about you." Everyone else nods their heads in a display of unity and deep concern. "You work too hard," your friend continues. "We think it might start affecting your health if you don't slow down."

With friends like that, who needs competitors? The fact is, they don't give a rip about your health. They just don't want to be embarrassed and outshone by comparison to your performance. That's their problem. That's their mountain to climb. You need to get over it and get on with your business. The more you focus on the squeaky wheels in your selling process and not the whiny wheels around the office the more sales and money you're going to make. Focus on pushing back the boundaries of your comfort zone instead of being recruited to protect their collective comfort zones.

Those worthwhile things that matter most usually aren't easy to obtain, anyway. Anybody who advises you to slow down or lighten up is not your friend. When you think about it, people who advise you to back off are telling you what to value and what to not value. Your commitment to practice will be automatic as long as you are clear about what you want and why you want it. We aren't suggesting that you must love every aspect of your job. But you must love the opportunities your job gives you.

Focusing on opportunities outside of yourself and the usual office crowd make the practicing seem worthwhile. The opportunity of creating a life of choice, contribution, and fulfillment to your family and community is enough to keep most folks going. Those are the opportunities that your job provides. Your success is ultimately unimportant except for the impact it has on others. Success may be meaningless if considered outside the context of contribution.

Get out there and practice. Practice by doing. Practice early and practice often. PEPO is an umbrella principle that encompasses CECO and AEAO. Be willing to fail your way to the top, because the view from the top will be much more pleasant if you climb long and hard to reach it. A helicopter ride to the summit is not quite as satisfying. Do the work. Prepare, anticipate obstacles, make adjustments quickly, and have fun along the way. Making mistakes is okay as long as you correct them and move on, with your principal task leading the way like a carrot on a stick.

FINAL LESSONS FROM CHILDREN

Practice like you used to when you were a kid. Life was a constant rehearsal and rehearsal was life. You tried everything. Kids are not prudent enough to sit and ponder what works and what doesn't. They just keep practicing until they get it right. They just do it until the dam breaks and they get what they want. Adulthood can be similar.

Hopefully you'll take a slightly more sophisticated approach, but not lose that never-say-die attitude in the process. It never occurs to kids that they might fall.

Only as people get older does the chance of failing slow them down. Kids are not familiar with the fear of failure. Fear of not having what they want is extremely real, however. There's a difference. The possibility of being told "No," and all of the catastrophized implications of rejection that go with it, will make adults shrink away from asking for anything. Kids don't sweat the word "No." Their only fear is doing without whatever it is they want so desperately. That's why their asking is so relentless. If there is anything for us to ultimately relearn from our childhoods it's to extract the venom from those two little letters, N and O. Defang or neuter them, but do whatever you must do to remove their power and influence to stop you from doing the things that will get you where you want to go and the things you want to take with you.

PERSONALITY-BASED PRACTICE

As always, it's important to consider who it is you're practicing on and what you're practicing for. Sports teams have two kinds of practice. The first is basic skills and fundamentals of the game. Salespeople need to practice and bone up on basics as much as athletes do. Then comes the specific practice for each different opponent. That's why coaches and players watch game films. They can review their mastery or lack of mastery for the game in general, and make specific adjustments and game plans for individual opponents, to address and counter the individual strengths, weaknesses, obstacles, and threats each one presents.

Practice for Machiavellians

Watching game films of a Machiavellian will reveal the patterns we've been describing throughout this book. Everything they do is part of a focused agenda to reach the top. You should therefore practice being an asset to their ascent and avoiding the appearance of being an obstacle. Practice following their lead in conversation, not holding to your own opinion about how they should do things. Practice seeing the world through someone else's eyes, since the view through the Machiavellian's eyes is likely to be quite different from your own. When you enter the world of the Machiavellian you don't need to become one. You need to understand them and what makes them tick. Practicing for Machiavellians, as with any other personality type, is very specific preparation.

Practice for Sadists

It will require a lot of practice to keep your own concepts of justice and fair treatment to yourself as you focus on how the value and benefits of your product will empower the sadist. His or her personal and professional agendas are his or her business, not yours. Practice detaching from the outcomes of what others do. Focus only on the good you can do for others. Obviously, you could reach some moral and ethical crossroads if the sadist is too over the top. That becomes a question of conscience for you. Assuming you're not a sadist, your primary practice must be to make what you're selling resonate with what the sadist wants, regardless of how foreign that is to you.

Practice for Masochists

The same principle of detachment applies to the masochist. You probably won't understand at a deep and visceral level why masochists feel they deserve to fail. Nor do you want to help them fail. You want to help them and those within their spheres of influence succeed. How the masochist interprets that success emotionally is beyond your control. You must practice relating information to the masochists you sell to in such a way as not to push them toward the edges of their comfort zones, even though you're probably way outside of yours just dealing with them. With masochists, as with any current or prospective customer, practice hitting them dead center in their comfort zone. It could be called "target" practice.

Practice for Paranoids

Paranoids have bizarre comfort zones. Practice hard. Everything you do will come under suspicion. You could even practice being suspicious of yourself before you meet face-to-face with a paranoid current or prospective customer. Practice your pitch by asking yourself, "Would I believe this if somebody approached me this way? Or would it arouse my suspicion?" Most people are paranoid to one degree or another when they encounter a salesperson, because experience has taught them that what is being said is intended to manipulate and lead to behavior other than what's being discussed. They don't know that you're above all that. Practice using honesty to put people at ease. Paranoids listen to people who have proven themselves trustworthy.

Practice for Greek Gods or Goddesses

As in the case of the Machiavellian you really need to practice getting your ego out of the way when dealing with small-g gods and goddesses. If you think you have a better idea you'd better be able to convince them that it's their idea. Practicing your humility and submission will prepare you to approach these small-d deified individuals. It will be a constant temptation to reveal that the emperor has no clothes on. If you give in to that temptation we hope you'll consider it reward enough for you and your skinny kids to laugh your heads off as you drive by the Greek god and goddess's mansions in that smoke machine you call a car.

Practice for Your Best Buddy

Your new best friend will enjoy practicing with you all day long. You can use your time with your best buddy to try things others wouldn't necessarily tolerate. "Let me try this on you," you say to your buddy customer. "What would you say if I told you that your face will shrivel up and fall off if you don't buy my product?"

"I'd say you're a laugh riot," your best buddy chuckles. "But my boss would have security remove you from the building." Your new best friends might be more friendly and useful than you gave them credit for. They'll cut you beaucoup slack where more mainstream, suspicious customers will give you one or two strikes before having security remove you from the premises. Practice on friendly audiences.

Practice for Decent Souls

Decent souls will also cut you a lot of slack, but they're too emotionally mature to let you practice on them for long. Their time is too important. They might say, "Come back and run that by me again after you work out the kinks in your presentation." That would be a tremendous act of charity and tolerance on their part. If you're so lucky as to have such customers, don't disappoint them. Leave, practice like crazy, polish your presentation, and then come back and impress the snot out of them. That will make them respect you for (1) listening and (2) following through. Take quality feedback, use it to refine your approach, and you're likely to hear, "Well done. Where do I sign?"

CHAPTER TWELVE SUMMARY

Practice is action. Your best practice is in doing. What makes it practice is the learning that's going on while you ply your trade. The more learning you do the sharper your skills become. It starts and ends with practice, practice, and more practice. You can never become too good at selling unless you have all the money you'll ever need or want, as well as everything your little heart desires. If you don't, practice.

- Never too good to practice: If professional and world-class amateur athletes need to practice to the very end of their competitive careers, why would you be any different? If virtuoso musicians practice even after their concert days are over, what's the lesson for the sales professional? It's clear that these people make practice and continuous improvement part of their lifestyle, right along with eating, sleeping, and perhaps making little virtuosos. The best people at anything become better with practice.
- There's no quit in practice: Champion runners, swimmers, and race car drivers don't quit a lap before the end of the race and coast the rest of the way. Where do you get off coasting toward the finish line? Some of the most colossal implosions in the history of sports followed an individual or team convincing themselves that the game was won before time expired. When time finally did expire so did the complacent competitors. It's not over until there are zeros on the clock.
- Practice overcomes cluelessness: You don't need to be the smartest to score the highest on the test. You don't need to be

the fastest to win the race. You don't need to be the most talented to sell the most records. You don't need to be the tallest to jump the highest. Twentieth century sports journalist Damon Runyon expanded on the Old Testament book of Ecclesiastes, chapter nine, verse 11, when he said, "The race is not always to the swift, nor the battle to the strong, but that's the way to bet." (Runyon's biography is at brainyencyclopedia .com) You might not be the fastest, strongest, or the brightest bulb in the box, but you can beat the odds with practice.

- Change the tire that's flat: Too often we catch ourselves changing a tire that's perfectly good instead of changing the flat. That's because it's easier to jack up any corner of the car except the one that's sitting on the pavement. It's not good enough to say, "I'm practicing constantly," if your practice ignores the areas where you need the most growth. The practice that's hardest to bring yourself to do will do you the most good.

- Friend or foe: If you begin practicing harder at sharpening your selling skills, your peers and colleagues will likely urge you to slow down lest you damage your health. What they're really asking you to do is slow down lest you damage their egos. Your true friends are those who will cheer you on as you invest the hard work and perseverance to get better at what you do. Anyone who discourages that is not your friend.

- Practice early and often: Make sure that you adjust your practice methods and techniques to reflect the uniqueness of your individual customers and their variable circumstances. Constant practice in the context of your different customers' individual needs will allow you to make specific adjustments and game plans to accommodate the individual strengths, weaknesses, obstacles, and threats each one represents.

Selling to an idiot isn't difficult as long as your inner idiot is not in charge. Selling to a genius will be a disaster if your inner idiot is in charge. Because of the natural disparity of power a current or prospective customer has over the sales professional, enormous compensations must be made through superior knowledge, ability to communicate, persistence, and passion.

Practicing these and every specific skill needed to sharpen your scalpel will put you in the driver's seat, no matter how bright or dull your customers are. At some point and at some level your inner idiot and your customer's inner idiot share the same space in the universe. That's the place from which to begin applying all of that natural and acquired talent and knowledge you continue to accumulate and refine. Remember, the tougher they are, the more they're likely to buy. Go in peace and sell their socks off.

INDEX